D1739313

The Telecommunications-Transportation Tradeoff

The Telecommunications- Transportation Tradeoff

Options for Tomorrow

by

JACK M. NILLES

and

F. ROY CARLSON JR.
PAUL GRAY
GERHARD J. HANNEMAN

A Wiley-Interscience Publication

JOHN WILEY & SONS

New York / London / Sydney / Toronto

Copyright © 1976 by John Wiley & Sons, Inc.

Library of Congress Cataloging in Publication Data:

Main entry under title:

The Telecommunications-transportation tradeoff.

"A Wiley-Interscience publication."
Includes bibliographical references and index.
1. Telecommunication.   2. Electronic data processing.
I. Nilles, Jack M.

HE7651.T44   384   76-18107
ISBN 0-471-01507-5

Printed in the United States of America

10 9 8 7 6 5 4 3 2 1

Preface

This book documents a research program begun in 1973 by an inter-disciplinary team of researchers at the University of Southern California. The research was initiated by a grant from the Research Applied to National Needs (RANN) Program of the National Science Foundation (Grant No. 39019). This book is an expansion and revision of the final report for that project, entitled "Final Report: Development of Policy on the Telecommunications-Transportation Tradeoff" (NSF-RA-5-74-020, December 1974). The research, which is continuing beyond the NSF-supported segment, has as its purpose the investigation of the public policy aspects of potential telecommunications alternatives to transportation.

PURPOSE

This work, because of its broad implications, is intended for reading by a varied audience. The intent is to provide a general overview of some of the possibilities for substituting telecommunications for trans-portation, and of the societal implications of widespread adoption of the substitutes.

The case study approach is used to provide some practical exam-ples of substitutions that are feasible today, and to illuminate areas where more information is needed. Technical details are included only to the extent necessary to establish the validity of the concepts presented.

The ultimate objective is to develop in readers with many different backgrounds an appreciation of some of the alternatives to the devel-opments in contemporary society made possible by technologies that are here, or almost here, today. A further objective is to demonstrate that our traditional ways of conducting our lives do not necessarily provide the best course of action. Finally, we hope to show that although newly developed technologies have enabled mankind to get itself into various forms of serious trouble, they can also be used to get us out of future difficulties. As problems of urban growth, energy shortages, and transportation congestion continue to worsen, these alternatives will achieve increasing importance and recognition. We hope that the reader will use this book to form a basis for his or her own thinking about using and developing technology for the wisest service to mankind. The choice is ours.

THE AUTHORS

Because of its scope this book raises many issues that question conventional ways of looking at the world and discusses them from many points of view. For this reason the research supporting this volume required the cooperation and expertise of representatives of a number of disciplines. Jack M. Nilles, Director of Interdisciplinary Program Development for the University, was the principal investigator for the project. He directed and coordinated the research from its inception, performed the energy analyses and transportation cost estimates, formulated and/or integrated the impact and policy analyses, and was responsible for most of the actual writing and final editing of this book. Frederic R. Carlson, an Assistant Dean of the School of Engineering; Paul Gray, of the Graduate School of Business Administration and a Senior Research Associate of its Center for Futures Research; and Gerhard J. Hanneman, Director of the Center for Communications Policy Research in the Annenberg School of Communications at USC, were coprincipal investigators. Dr. Carlson directed research on the technological aspects of the telecommunications–transportation tradeoff; his work included design of a model telecommunications network, scenario formulation, and cost calculations for various technological alternatives. Dr. Gray was responsible for the identification and analysis of the economic aspects of the tradeoff. Under his direction case studies were performed of a large insurance company and the general banking industry. The study of the insurance company included the collection of data on the organization and definition of the information flow patterns between various sectors of the company. Dr. Hanneman coordinated research on the motivational aspects of the tradeoff. In particular, this involved the design, administration, and analysis of a series of surveys of various populations to determine their perceptions of a telecommunications–transportation tradeoff. The entire team was continuously involved in integrating most of the aspects of the research, making it truly a joint project.

ACKNOWLEDGMENTS

Many individuals participated in the conduct of the research and the preparation of this book. Dr. Jack Munushian, Chairman of the Computer Science Program at USC, participated in the project throughout and provided valuable advice and information regarding the USC Interactive Instructional Television System. His counsel is greatly appreciated. We are also indebted to Ken Down, Director of the IITV System at Stanford University, for his cooperation. The research assistants from the School of Engineering, James Cochran and Lorraine del'Osso, participated in the definition of the technological and communications network requirements. David Lopez, from the Graduate School of Business Administration, worked extensively on definition of the company's organizational configuration, evaluation of the company's communication requirements, and compilation of employee transportation data. Thomas Dubanoski, Maissa Ibrahim, and Marie Jurusz participated in the survey design, administered the survey instruments, and analyzed the resulting data. Maggie Cross, aided by Leslie Rugg, undertook the difficult, frustrating, and tedious task of compiling and editing the primary draft of the book. Janna Wong, who came to the program as a computer-naive individual, ably demonstrated that it is possible to train people in a short time to interact with computers. She compiled the final manuscript of the book by using an interactive computer-editing system.

In addition to those already named, who were directly involved in the research, the team is indebted to many others who were instrumental in providing information and encouragement. Some of the most notable of these are Dr. Allen Shinn, of the National Science Foundation, who was the NSF's program manager for the project; the executive officers and staff of the insurance company, who provided the data for our case study; Dr. Alex Reid, of the British Post Office; Dr. Richard Harkness, now with Stanford Research Institute; and Mr. Sam Clawson, formerly of the Planning Department of Santa Barbara County, who first piqued Jack Nilles' interest in the concept of telecommunications substitutes for travel, early in 1971. Mr. Clawson's paper on the subject, "Is Transportation Obsolete?" was presented to the CONFER-IN of the American Institute of Planners in Minneapolis/St. Paul, Minnesota, in October, 1970.

CAVEAT

The opinions expressed herein are those of the authors and not necessarily those of any of the organizations with which the authors have been associated or which have otherwise participated in our research.

Jack M. Nilles
F. Roy Carlson, Jr.
Paul Gray
Gerhard J. Hanneman

Los Angeles, California
May 1976

Contents

Chapter 1

Background

Just after the turn of the century, in a story entitled "The Machine Stops," E. M. Forster depicted a telecommunications dominated world of the future [1.1]. Designed to rescue mankind from a hopelessly polluted and ravaged world, the "machine" housed people underground and provided for their physical needs through the use of such things as a worldwide communications network, videophones, central data files, voice activated machines, and high-speed printers. Because society became totally dependent on the machine without knowing how to repair it, the inevitable breakdown of the machine resulted in the demise of most of humanity. At the time the story was written, such technological wonders were fantasy; today, they are becoming accepted as commonplace by many Americans. Telecommunications technologies are becoming ubiquitous and powerful.

Yet, until recently in the history of man, communication over any distance was dependent upon transportation, that is, one had to physically travel or send written documents to another place to communicate with another individual or to transact business. To a large degree the availability of varieties of transportation determined the location, growth, and configuration of cities. In the seventeenth, eighteenth, and nineteenth centuries the locations of most American cities at the conjunction of waterways or near natural harbors satisfied the transportation and communication needs of the inhabitants. Railroads and the telegraph permitted the growth of cities on the Great Plains at the conjunction of or along major overland trade routes. By the end of the nineteenth century, a new phenomenon—urban sprawl—was developing as a consequence of the introduction of the electric streetcar. The automobile aggravated and institutionalized the growth of suburbia.

Today, suburbia continues to push outward into rural areas while the city cores become more business oriented. R. C. Harkness modeled the resulting configuration as a series of concentric zones [1.2]. In the center is the central business district, consisting of offices and retail stores. This is surrounded by a deteriorating zone of railroad terminals, older manufacturing plants, and warehouses. The next zone comprises older, high-density residential areas that are declining into slums in many cities. The remaining zones represent newer housing developments, usually of single-family dwellings, that have been built since World War II and the spread of the private automobile. A major factor behind the development of these zones is the city-center oriented, radial highway and rail transportation system.

Every major city in the United States has one or more central business districts (CBD's) strung together with freeways. A recent Department of Transportation report entitled "Suburbanization and Its Implications for Urban Transportation Systems" noted that 46% of the metropolitan population lives in the urban fringe and that the recent trend is toward a mixture of high- and low-density areas in the fringe [1.3]. The urban fringes of most metropolitan areas are now developing a series of higher-density business and government "activity clusters." These, combined with the existing high-density CBD's, portend a broad metropolitan area comprising high-density nodes surrounded by lower-density residential areas. As the metropolitan areas continue to expand we are faced with the new phenomenon of megalopoli extending over vast areas of land and presenting unique transportation problems. The inherently low population density of this urban sprawl is in itself a major cause of extensive transportation usage. The fact that the average metropolitan worker lives at some distance from his work exacerbates the problem.

URBAN TRANSPORTATION

The ubiquitous private automobile dominates urban transportation and has major impacts on the structure of urban life. In 1970, 92 million automobiles were registered in the United States, or 10 for every 23 people [1.4]. Approximately 63 million of these automobiles (representing the 68.2% of the population that lives in urban areas) [1.5] are in metropolitan areas. Victor Gruen, a noted urban planner, estimates that the space required for private automobiles in a typical city is more than six times as great as the living space required for the inhabitants [1.6]. By 1969 motor vehicles accounted for 77% (by weight) of the more than 87 million tons of carbon monoxide emitted annually in the United States, 50% of the 25 million tons of hydrocarbons, and 33% of the 18 million tons of nitrogen oxides [1.7]. In urban areas automobiles contribute an even higher percentage of pollutants, typically producing more than 90% of the carbon monoxide and up to 75% of the hydrocarbons [1.8].

The energy costs of private automobiles are high, both in terms of effectiveness when compared with other modes of urban mass transportation and of the total energy used in the United States. Estimates of total energy costs for transportation range from 23.8% to 25.2% of the gross national energy use [1.9, 1.10]. This proportion of gross national energy use is expected to remain relatively constant for the next few years. This amounts to 17 Quad (quadrillion British Thermal Units) of energy used in 1971 for transportation with an expected 19 Quad in 1975.

Automobile transportation constitutes 42% of all transportation use, according to Hirst [1.11]. Urban automobile use accounted for 34.2% of all transportation use in 1970, or 5.6 Quad [1.12]. We estimate an urban automobile usage of 36.7% of all transportation in 1975. Using the above estimates for total transportation use, this amounts to 9.2% of the total U.S. energy consumption for 1975 for urban automobile use.

Approximately 42% of all urban automobile transportation is for the purpose of commuting to work or other work-related trips [1.13]. This usage amounts to 3.9% of the total U.S. energy consumption, or 15.4% of U.S. transportation energy consumption. If these percentages of usage remain constant, commuting will account for 2.9 Quad in 1975. Thus, each percent reduction in urban commuting could result in a total increase in U.S. energy conservation of about 30 trillion Btu or 8.6 billion kilowatt-hours annually. The average U.S. household was expected to consume 9730 kilowatt-hours in 1975 [1.14]. Thus a 1% reduction in commuting would save enough fuel energy to supply the residential electricity needs of a medium-sized city.

In addition to the energy required to commute, the commuting mode has also required the construction of major urban highway systems in most metropolitan areas. These systems are both inefficient (in terms of their variable loading) and costly to build and maintain. The other transit options—widespread bus networks and/or fixed rail transit— are similarly costly and suffer from the same problems of variable loading. A dilemma clearly exists. Although most major American cities have become dependent upon efficient and/or popular forms of transportation, escalating costs, energy shortages, traffic congestion, and pollution may preclude total adherence to traditional transportation modes. Other alternatives must be considered.

AN OPTION—TELECOMMUTING

In considering ways to alleviate commuter traffic, we find that one factor may be critical: the type of work the commuter performs. Some work requires the physical presence of the worker at or near an immovable object or central location. Examples are the creation of physical goods in factories, the transfer of physical goods, or the performance of a service requiring face-to-face meetings. Such work is heavily transportation dependent, and it is difficult to foresee alternatives to transportation for workers engaged in these industries.

However, in parallel with the advent and growth of electronic and computer technologies, an increasing proportion of the population has been engaged in the creation, transfer, processing and/or storage of information—work that does not necessarily require the physical presence of the worker. Nonetheless, these "information industry" workers are still required to commute to and from central locations in major business districts. Given the capability of modern telecommunications and computer technologies to efficiently produce, transmit, and store information, it appears probable that many information industry workers could "telecommute." That is, they could perform their work, using communications and computer technologies, at locations much closer to their homes than is the case now. If telecommuting could be shown to be feasible, an alternative to commuting would be available to a significant portion of the central business district labor force. It was this possibility that the USC research group considered, with the aim of defining the critical elements of the substitution and identifying the key policy areas associated with the substitution of telecommunications for transportation.

The term "tradeoff" denotes a key concept in this research. As used here "tradeoff" refers to the process of evaluating the various alternative approaches to accomplishing a given task or goal, weighing their relative merits, and selecting the "best" one. The "best" approach is the one that most nearly satisfies the objectives of the individual or organization making the decision to implement the alternative.

Historically the tradeoff at the individual or organizational level is concerned only with the immediate and direct costs and benefits of each alternative. The indirect effects of an alternative frequently have been ignored by the decision maker. For example, an individual in buying a car is concerned mainly with trading the direct benefits (style, status, performance, carrying capacity, etc.) against the direct cost (down payment, monthly payments) of purchase. The indirect costs (additional depletion of fossil fuel resources, increases in air pollution and traffic congestion, diversion of mineral resources from other applications, etc.) are considered only occasionally in this decision. Thus the consideration of the central public policy issue during the research: How should public policy be altered, if at all, to ensure that tradeoff decisions made at the individual or organizational level have a net public as well as a net private benefit?

PREMISES

The core questions of our research were: Can telecommunications and computer technologies be substituted for some portion of urban commuter traffic? Can such a substitution reduce commuter congestion and mitigate the major economic impacts of new commuter-oriented transportation systems? What are the possible societal impacts of the substitution? What policy questions should be considered at the federal, state, regional, and local levels? The research emphasis was placed on the evaluation of three primary aspects of the telecommunications-transportation substitution.

Economic Incentives

A key premise in the research was that the prospects for substitution of telecommuting for commuting would be greatest where individual business firms or government agencies could perceive clear economic advantages to dispersing their labor forces from central business districts. Existence of this economic advantage is a necessary, if not sufficient, condition for the decision by an individual firm or agency to engage in telecommuting.

To evaluate the potential economic incentive, the team performed a preliminary case study of a typical information industry firm and evaluated for this firm the costs and benefits of telecommunications as an alternative to transportation.

Technological Base

It was apparent that a sufficiently advanced technological base was required to meet the work-related communications requirements of the firm. Therefore the team defined the communication requirements of the information industry firm, developed a series of work scenarios, assessed available technology in the context of the firm's requirements, designed a hypothetical communications network for the company, and performed a preliminary cost/benefit analysis.

Effectiveness

Since substitution is dependent on the ability of workers to perform their work in a telecommunications environment and their willingness to do so, the team attempted preliminary assessments of the effectiveness of the telecommuting mode.

A series of surveys was developed and given to USC and Stanford University students who had chosen telecommunications over transportation by using the Interactive Instructional Television Systems at their schools. The students' attitudes and motivations were studied. This portion of the research also required extensive background research into previous experiments on the effectiveness of telecommunications in various work environments.

SIGNIFICANCE

On the basis of the research the team developed estimates of some of the major economic and social impacts of the telecommunications option. The primary impacts were projected as the development or extension of telecommunications networks; a reduction in energy use and changes in the form of delivered energy; and changes in transportation planning, design, and growth. Areas of secondary impact are changes in urban growth and land use patterns; development of new modes of business; new options in resource conservation; and related societal structure alternatives.

The research team was concerned with questions of net societal benefit. If the net societal benefits are seen to be negative in either the long or the short term, then it is imperative that adequate government policies—on all levels—be developed to eliminate, forestall, or mitigate any undesirable effects, particularly where there is otherwise an economic incentive to individual firms to use telecommunications. On the other hand, where positive societal benefits will occur it is equally imperative that policies be developed, or existing policies be reinforced, to enhance the desired effects. It is particularly important for government agencies to be aware of the public policy issues related to the telecommunications option, particularly if, as postulated, individual organizations choose this option on the basis of their own self-interest—enlightened or otherwise.

The following chapters of this book treat the methods and results of the USC research and conclude with a discussion of some of the implications of the findings, particularly as they relate to public policy.

REFERENCES

1. E. M. Forster. "The Machine Stops." In *The Eternal Moment*. New York: Harcourt, Brace and Company, 1928.

2. R. C. Harkness. "Communications Substitutes for Travel: A Preliminary Assessment of their Potential for Reducing Urban Transportation Costs by Altering Office Location Patterns." Ph.D. dissertation, University of Washington, Ann Arbor: University Microfilms, 1973, p. 267.

3. U.S. Department of Transportation. *Suburbanization and its Implications for Urban Transportation Systems*. Washington, D.C.: U.S. Department of Transportation, Office of the Assistant Secretary for Systems Development and Technology, Office of R&D Policy, 1974, p. 1.

4. U.S. Bureau of the Census. *Statistical Abstract of the United States*. Washington, D.C.: Government Printing Office, 1972.

5. *Ibid.*, p. 16.

6. Victor Gruen. *Centers for the Urban Environment: Survival of the Cities*. New York: Van Nostrand Reinhold Company, 1973, p. 163.

7. Eric Hirst. *Energy Intensiveness of Passenger and Freight Transport Modes: 1960–1970*. Oak Ridge: Oak Ridge National Laboratory, ORNL-NSF Environmental Program, 1973, p. 23.

8. American Society for Engineering Education. *Interdisciplinary Research Topics in Urban Engineering: A report by the Urban Engineering Study Committee of the American Society for Engineering Education*. Washington, D.C.: American Society for Engineering Education, October 1969, pp. 198–199.

9. *Ibid.*, p. 200.

10. Ford Foundation Energy Policy Project. *Exploring Energy Choices*. Washington, D.C.: Ford Foundation Energy Policy Project, 1974, p. 69. This reference is drawn from a report issued by Stanford Research Institute, "Patterns of Energy Consumption in the United States," prepared for the Office of Science and Technology, Office of the President, Washington, D.C., 1972.

11. Hirst, *op. cit.*, p. 24.

12. *Ibid.*

13. Automobile Manufacturers Association, Inc. *1971 Automobile Facts and Figures*. Detroit: Automobile Manufacturers Association, Inc., 1971, p. 52.

14. *Electrical World*. September 15, 1969, p. 90.

Chapter 2

The Information Industry

For the purposes of this exposition, *a component of the information industry is defined as any economic activity that is primarily involved in the storage, transfer, or manipulation of information.* Typical information industry members are: insurance companies, accountant firms, stockbrokers, and others in the financial and banking sector; educational institutions; the media; administrative operations of organizations, regardless of the organization's primary economic activity; and those government agencies or agency components where the primary activity is information transfer. Less typical members of the information industry are those manufacturing firms that have largely automated their facilities through the use of numerically controlled machine tools and similar process controls that can be remotely located from the machine.

GENERAL CHARACTERISTICS

Many of the employees of information industry firms currently travel to and from locations in central business districts every day to interact with some form of communications or storage system such as a computer, the mail, or a physical filing system. Many of these jobs do not inherently require frequent face-to-face interaction with other persons or the performance of physical services necessitating a common central location. Currently, about half of the United States' labor force comprises white-collar workers [2.1], the great majority of whom are in information industries or information segments of other industries. The white-collar segment of the labor force is the fastest growing segment in the United States. It has been forecast that white-collar workers will increase from the level of 38.0 million in 1970 to 48.8 million in 1980, an annual growth rate of 2.5% [2.2]. For the same period, the annual growth rate for the United States population (205 million to 223 million) and the labor force (85.9 million to 102.5 million) is expected to be only 0.9% and 1.8% respectively [2.3].

Specifically, Table 2.1 shows a rough estimate of the number of clerical or equivalent information industry workers in 1970. The estimate was made by examining the 1973 Statistical Abstract and estimating the fraction of the personnel in each reported industry who reasonably could be said to concern themselves primarily with routine information processing activities. This conservative estimate of roughly 7.9 million information industry *routine* workers can be compared with a figure of 13.7 million "clerical and kindred" workers counted in

Table 2.1. Information Industry Employment Estimates, 1970[a]

Type	Total in Category (× 1000)	Estimated Clerical and related non-supervisory (× 1000)	Source Table
Federal Civilian (white collar)	2113	634[b]	637
State & local government (white collar)		2500	674
Banking, finance & insurance		2900	364
Miscellaneous business services		644[c]	364
Transportation & public utilities (8% of total employment)		366	364
Printing & Publishing (15% of total employment)		166	364
Manufacturing, durables (6% of total)		672	

Total clerical and equivalent information industries employment: 7,876,000

[a] Source: *Statistical Abstracts,* 1973
[b] GS–3 and below, at 30% of total white-collar workers
[c] 40% of 1.6 × 10^6

the 1970 census [2.4]. Thus at least 10%, and possibly 17%, of the total U.S. work force of 78.6 million are in this category.

Furthermore, the growth rate of the clerical worker segment of the economy between 1950 and 1970 was exceeded only by the rate of increase of professional, technical, and kindred workers, most of whom are members of information industries. If we add the total of the white-collar worker categories for 1970, including managers, officials, proprietors, and sales workers we arrive at a figure of 38 million or 48.3% of the total work force. These components of the 1950 to 1970 growth rate of this sector, when linearly extrapolated to the year 2000, yields an estimated white-collar work force that is roughly 55% of the total. Since much of the growth in this area is exponential rather than linear, this is probably a conservative estimate.

Aside from the large and growing set of information industries, the important issue here concerns the possibility for reexamining and reevaluating the ways in which these workers perform their jobs to arrive at estimates of some alternative futures for them. Central to this issue are the following questions:

1.   What information is passed on, altered, or produced by each worker?

2.   How frequent are these transfer events?

3.   Who, or what, is the immediate recipient of the information produced?

Some related questions are: What is now the mode of the information transfer (e.g., written messages, face-to-face conversations, graphic displays, interactive, or one way, TV)? How effective is that mode? Could other modes using telecommunications be more effective; in what ways and in what circumstances? The research to be described here concentrated on exploring specific cases where these questions were asked.

Much of the research to date on telecommunications substitutes for travel has concentrated on the efficacy of telecommunications and computer technologies in the conduct of management operations within the information (and other) industries (see the Appendix). Many questions have been raised concerning the suitability of various modes of telecommunications for the conduct of management functions. Our research, although recognizing that many questions raised in these areas are important, placed its emphasis on examination of the potential utility of telecommuting for the clerical and middle management workers in these industries, who together constitute the major portion of the labor force in the information industry. The economic and societal impacts of a conversion to telecommuting for this group could have far greater consequences than a similar conversion by management personnel. It should be noted, however, that the decision on the part of the individual firms to make this substitution could conceivably be based on a disproportionately high emphasis on its perceived utility to members of management.

EVOLUTIONARY PHASES

Before discussing the detailed characteristics of a member of the information industry, it is instructive to consider a potential evolutionary organizational process for information industry firms. Our somewhat arbitrary definitions of the steps in this process illustrate the major phases an organization may undergo in terms of its geographical structure and corresponding telecommunications and transportation interfaces.

Four evolutionary phases or forms of organizational structures were identified as they relate to the potential modes of applications of telecommunications technology and their effect on public policy. These phases are: *centralization, fragmentation, dispersion, and diffusion.*

Centralization

Centralization represents the current dominant mode in most industries. All administrative operations are located at a single site, with workers divided into functional groups according to their primary information product. Where national organizations divide into regional officies, the regional home office generally replicates this monolithic structure. Both Corporations A and B are centralized in Figure 2.1a.

Fragmentation

In this phase *coherent* subunits of the central organization break off and relocate elsewhere. The communications boundaries of the organization are stretched and replaced by telecommunications or mail, but the communications within the unit remain intact. Two common variations of fragmentation are *branching*, such as occurs in banks where the fragmented unit is a miniature replica of the parent, and *segmenting*, where functional units such as data processing, accounting, or

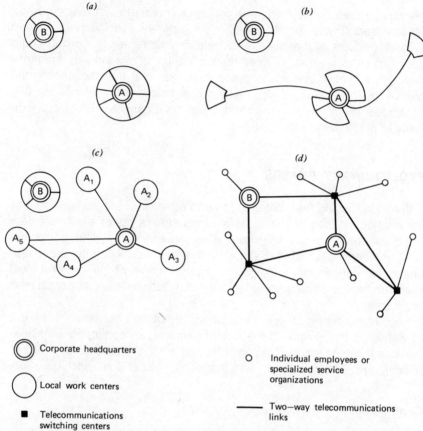

Figure 2.1 Organizational evolution—two cases, Corporation A and B. (a) Centralization; (b) fragmentation; (c) dispersion; (d) diffusion.

marketing are separated from the central core (Corporation A in Figure 2.1b).

Unfortunately, because of the great availability and relatively low cost of the private automobile, in the past fragmentation has generally increased, rather than decreased, commuting. This can be seen from the experience of many medium-sized cities such as Atlanta, Georgia, Washington, D.C., or Boston, Massachusetts, where a beltway has been built around the city. New commercial centers, including segments or branches of central organizations, spring up along the beltway, particularly at the intersections with freeways that lead downtown. People who live on one part of the perimeter apparently tend to work, by the perversity of human nature, on an opposite part of the perimeter. Furthermore, many people who live inside the perimeter travel through downtown to reach their places of work. The net effect has been to increase the downtown congestion beyond that which would result from the growth of downtown office space itself, because of the large number of people who pass through. In Los Angeles, for example, only 42% of the people who travel into the downtown freeway interchanges actually stop in the CBD [2.6].

As an example of fragmenting, we can study a typical centralized organization, one that has been in the same location for many years. An examination of the locations of its employees' residences will show that a large number of them live fairly close to the organization, with decreasing numbers as the distance from the office increases (i.e., roughly a circular normal distribution). Thus, the center of mass of the organization's employee population is at the same location as the organizational headquarters. Local geography may affect this distribution somewhat, but it otherwise seems intuitively appropriate. Our case study verifies this general configuration (see Chapter 3).

What happens when the organization fragments? The new location or locations of the organization's coherent subunits now constitute new centers to which the employees must commute. At least initially, the average employee must travel to work farther than before since the new locations are not at the centroid of the residential distribution but are scattered within the distribution. The key element in the organizational structure that makes this so is that the relocated subunits are coherent, that is, the accounting department (or the computer department, warehouse operations, etc.) moves en masse to the new location. Thus, although the accounting department employee residences can be expected to be fairly uniformly scattered throughout the residential area of the organization, the employees themselves must now converge daily to a single, now noncentral point.

In contemporary business situations, the general organizational reaction to this phenomenon is either to pay moving expenses for some employees, typically those who live more than some minimum distance from work, or to allow attrition of the newly distant work force (resulting from disgruntled employees finding jobs elsewhere) and hire local replacements for those who leave, or some combination of these. This process can often have serious consequences on the efficiency of the operation during the transition period. The management decision to relocate generally involves a weighing of the adverse factors of fragmentation, such as those listed above, with the positive benefits of relocation, many of which will be discussed in later chapters. The influence of telecommunications in making a fragmented operation effective derives mainly from its ability to maintain effective interdepartmental (i.e., interlocational) communications.

Dispersion

The third stage of decentralization is dispersion. In dispersion, as in fragmentation, the firm establishes a number of work locations throughout the city. However, employees now report to the location *nearest their homes, irrespective of the department in which they work* (Corporation A in Figure 2.1c; Corporation B is still centralized). The employees obtain their operating information through the "central" computer, either directly or through local minicomputer or file storage. Supervision and coordination activities make much greater use of communications and computer, rather than line-of-sight, interaction than in either of the previous two evolutionary stages.

In a fragmented operation, business tends to be carried out much as if the subunit were centralized. This is because most of the intraorganizational communications in the accounting or other fragmented departments are carried out primarily within the department. Hence no major new communications problems arise, or if they do, they tend to be concentrated more at interdepartmental and higher management than at the clerical levels. In a dispersed organization, on the other hand, since the "accounting department" now consists of a collection of employees whose work sites are physically scattered around the city, the communications problems can be significant.

In the dispersed situation, either the jobs of the employees must be redesigned so that they can still be self-contained at each individual location, or a sufficiently sophisticated telecommunications and information storage system must be developed to allow the information transfer to occur as effectively as if the employees were centrally collocated. For example, a supervisor in a dispersed organization can be one of two types: a local executive who provides physical supervision over the employees present at his location, regardless of the jobs they are performing; or a remote supervisor who is able to interrogate the activities of the employees in his department by means of a computer-mediated telecommunications system.

In dispersion those executives who require many and diverse face-to-face contacts to perform their jobs may still report to a central location to permit such interaction, but the great mass of clerical workers would be able to achieve substantial reductions in commuting. Even many of the executives might be able to confine their CBD visits to one or two days per week. Dispersion would also permit firms to tap labor markets that are not presently available; for example, housewives working while their children are in school, high school and college students in the late afternoons and others who have other jobs or are required for other reasons to keep nonstandard working hours.

Diffusion

The ultimate stage in this telecommunications catalyzed process is diffusion. In the diffusion stage, firms could maintain a relatively small core staff either dispersed or at a single location. Peaks in work load or special types of work would be handled by individual workers who offer their services through a telecommunications network to several different firms or clients (both corporations in Figure 2.1d). This particular phenomenon has already appeared without the use of tele communications in the form of companies that offer accounting, consulting, or temporary secretarial services and, of course, is common in the professions of law and medicine.

In a telecommunications diffused work society, the information service could be offered in at least two ways. The most likely in the near term involves development of specialty organizations that provide specific business information services to their clients through telecommunications links. Typical contemporary examples of this are firms that provide one or more business data services by means of interactive computer systems. These services range from provision of current stock market data to a network of brokerage houses to minor bookkeeping for small business firms. In these cases the service firm owns or leases its time-sharing computer, providing its services to an array of clients by means of a telecommunications system. The firm's employees report to a single location, if the firm is small. As the advantages of this new business operational flexibility become more apparent to the business community, more diverse services will be offered by this means.

One interesting example of a diffuse mode of operation, which presently involves the additional use of transportation, is provided by WESRAC, an Industrial Applications Center (IAC) at the University of Southern California, supported by the National Aeronautics and Space Administration. The primary purpose of WESRAC is to provide current information to industrial, educational, and governmental clients concerning technological progress. For this purpose, WESRAC has at its disposal a variety of computerized data bases. These data bases are physically located at a number of sites around the United States, and owned by a number of different organizations.

A popular service provided by WESRAC involves a data search

specialist traveling to client sites throughout the Los Angeles area. The specialist, equipped with a portable computer terminal, performs on-site data base searches for the client organizations on a scheduled periodic or ad hoc basis. The clients, generally small to medium-sized manufacturing organizations, would otherwise have no access to the information or would have to travel to and from WESRAC frequently to get the same service. Since the search specialist has access during a visit to all interested client personnel, either directly or through in-house conference telephones, the efficiency of the search session is generally much higher than would be the case if client representatives visited WESRAC. As the information industry develops, and more organizations require computer terminals with telecommunications capacity, even this interim, hybrid diffusion situation will largely eliminate the travel component.

The extreme case of diffusion is that in which the individual employee works at home, rather than at a local business center. It is this case which has received the most attention in the mass media. In principle, with technological and software capabilities now readily available or in an advanced state of development, there is no reason why many workers could not perform most or all of their duties from home. In practice, however, there are several technological and institutional barriers in contemporary society acting to prevent all but a few workers from working in this way.

One of the major technological and economic barriers to ultimate diffusion is the requirement for the widespread availability of switched data networks rather than the relatively small number of private dedicated networks or leased line systems used in dispersion. This is a problem of great technological complexity and involves major new capital investments. This factor, coupled with a variety of management considerations, makes it unlikely that the extreme stage of diffusion decentralization will be acceptable to many large organizations in the near future. However, the possibilities of the more concentrated mode of diffusion mentioned earlier may become increasingly attractive to the smaller, service-providing organizations which constitute a growing portion of society.

REFERENCES

1. U.S. Department of Labor. *Handbook of Labor Statistics.* Washington, D.C.: U.S. Department of Labor, Bureau of Labor Statistics, 1973, p. 39.
2. *Predicasts*, Issue 53, October 26, 1973, p. A–5. *Predicasts* is a news service

published by Predicasts, Inc., 200 University Circle Research Center, 11001 Cedar Avenue, Cleveland, Ohio, 44106.

3. *Ibid.*

4. U.S. Office of Management and Budget. *Social Indicators, 1973.* Washington, D.C.: Social and Economic Statistics Administration, U.S. Department of Commerce, p. 143.

5. U.S. Bureau of the Census. *Statistical Abstract of the United States.* Washington D.C.: U.S. Bureau of the Census, 1973.

6. Los Angeles City Traffic Department, Transportation Planning Division. *Staff Report: Home-to-Work Trip Making Characteristics of Vehicle Drivers and Bus Passengers for the "Cordon Count" Area.* Los Angeles, June 20, 1974, p. 7.

Chapter 3

Case Studies

Insurance and banking account for 3.6% of the gross national product of the United States (estimated at $41 billion in 1975) [3.1]; they provide typical examples of information industries. Most of the main regional business offices for these two industries are located in large central headquarters buildings in urban central business districts. The primary functions of most of the employees in banking and insurance companies are: (1) the recording of transactions; and (2) the updating of central, computer-kept files. The use of telecommunications and computer technologies (separately, if not jointly), is already widespread in these industries. An expansion of the joint uses of telecommunications and computer technologies to permit decentralization of these industries from urban central business districts, their prime locations for information handling, could have a significant impact on traffic congestion in urban areas.

Early in our research, a broad comparison was made between the banking and insurance industries. We found the two industries differed considerably in their data processing operations. The most notable difference was that insurance companies are centralized, "stand-alone" operations (where the record keeping of one company is completely independent of any other insurance company) while banking involves a combination of centralized, fragmented, and dispersed organizations and is a highly interdependent industry.

We postulated that decentralization, using telecommunications, could occur spontaneously if and when it becomes economically attractive to individual companies or groups of interrelated companies. The interdependent structure of the banking industry, depending as it does upon a complex network of financial reporting and document flow (especially physical transfer of checks), precluded a simple analysis of the process of further decentralization through adoption of telecommunications. Therefore a decision was made not to cover both industries in depth, but instead to perform a detailed analysis of an insurance company as a quicker way of estimating the feasibility of the telecommunications-transportation tradeoff. The preliminary analysis of the banking industry indicated that similar tradeoffs would occur, provided that the core problems of achieving a secure means of fund transfer (especially checks) operations were to be resolved first. This is discussed further at the end of this chapter.

INSURANCE COMPANY CASE

The research team contacted the western regional office of a major national insurance company to start development of data for the case study. Throughout the project the company has been extremely cooperative in providing information, the experience of key executives, and access to employees. Their cooperation in supplying employee and task data is gratefully acknowledged. By mutual agreement, the company is not named here. Nevertheless, examination of other companies in the industry leads the research team to believe that the factors presented here are typical of the industry.

Located in a central business district of Los Angeles, the company studied was faced with the problem that their building, over 25 years old, was becoming filled beyond its useful capacity and was beginning to show signs of age. For example, the air conditioning was incapable of coping with the cooling demands. Further, the neighborhood population had aged, and the insurance company was no longer able to find its labor force locally. The local management was aware that a decision regarding physical location of the regional office was imminent, and the telecommunications-transportation option was one they wished to explore.

The central management on the East Coast, although also interested in exploring the option, has a long-standing policy restricting the minimum size of any regional office to 1000 employees. Given this restriction, the Los Angeles management could only consider a fragmented configuration in the short term. Nevertheless, the Los Angeles management cooperated in an investigation of the possibilities for a dispersed network of offices linked by a telecommunications network. In fact, the company had already begun experimenting with small, satellite offices located at some distance from the central office in an attempt to test productivity factors.

The primary operations performed at the central or regional offices of most major insurance companies are: (1) underwriting of new policies; and (2) record keeping for existing policies. (This refers to central administrative offices—not the field offices which are primarily concerned with sales and initial processing of claims.) Since the number of policyholders is usually large, most companies now keep their records on computer files, using large clerical staffs to update the information in the machine. Hence, the primary work for a large portion of insurance company employees is computer-associated information processing.

The insurance company we studied conformed to this pattern. Large (IBM 370/155 and 360/65) computers served all the departments. The work of each department was centered around transforming its own particular type of input information into a form suitable for computer records. Even cursory analyses indicated that there was no technical need for the employees who transformed information for computer storage and the machines to be located in the same building. However, it was not initially clear what other organizational considerations existed that may have required the various groups to be housed centrally. We therefore undertook a study of (1) the organization of the insurance company, (2) the tasks performed by the employees, (3) their communication requirements, and (4) the equivalent characteristics of the newly established satellite offices of the company.

Organization

The labor force in the headquarters consisted of three distinct groups of employees: executives, middle management, and clerical workers. Executive categories included high line and staff positions and represented 6% of the staff. Middle management represented 27% of the total, including supervisors of clerical workers as well as functional specialists. The remaining 67% were clerical workers with job titles such as clerk typist, keypunch operator, and service clerk. A breakdown of these employees by job level, salary, and executive titles is given in Table 3.1. The element of greatest importance was the sizeable fraction of the labor force that was engaged in clerical work. These employees constituted the majority of the workers and did (as shown later) the majority of the traveling to work. Therefore we concentrated on investigating the requirements for, and the implications of, successfully substituting telecommunications for transportation for these workers. Most of them commute to the headquarters building located near the Los Angeles central business district (CBD). A few of the employees commute much shorter distances to two smaller satellite locations.

Table 3.1. Insurance Company Employees

Class	Level	Number	Subtotal	Salary/Week[a] (Median)	Title
	1	3		$103	
	2	197		108	
	3	424		115	
Clerical	4	402		123	
	5	384		135	
	6	278	1688	144	
	7	183		157	
	8	177		169	
	9	143		183	
	10	60		199	
	11	90		213	
	12	27	681	230	
	20	83			Associate Manager
	60	44			Manager
	77	8			Associate General Manager
	78	3			General Manager
	79	4			Director of Agencies
	80	4			Vice-President
	82	1			Vice-President
	84	1	148		Senior Vice-President
			2517		

[a] 1973 Data

The company is organized along typical pyramidal structure lines. The head of the regional office is a senior vice-president with four vice-presidents reporting to him, three concerned with such matters as investments, group insurance, and sales. The remaining vice-president is concerned with the administrative functions which constitute the primary activities of the central office (Figure 3.1). Because of the large number of clerical personnel involved, the research team focused its attention on the activities in the organizational elements under the administrative vice-president.

The insurance company fills its clerical positions primarily by hiring recent high school graduates. Thus, the company serves as an entry level employer. The company believes this practice has twofold benefits, first because it provides employees of sufficient skill at minimum cost. Second, the clerical workers constitute a nonunion labor force, which the company prefers. However, these advantages are offset by a very rapid turnover rate for clerical personnel (100% every three years) with a concomitant need for a large potential labor pool and consequent high training costs.

At middle management and executive levels the company provides job security, which increases with level until at the highest levels it is almost complete. Many of the employees at these levels were hired as clerical employees and have followed career paths within the company to attain their present positions. Because perceived career investment in the company also increases with time, and the company is in a stable industry, they tend to prefer staying with the company for their entire working careers.

The company provides several direct fringe benefits at its central building. These benefits include free parking, a slightly higher salary (relative to equivalent work in other areas of the city), free hot lunches, reduced insurance rates, a reduced (37½ hour) workweek, and a free annual physical examination. Identification of these benefits is important since the creation of decentralized regional offices could permit the company to reduce some or all of them. This would provide an economic incentive to the company. In fact, at its two experimental satellite locations the company has eliminated the first three of these benefits.

Communications Requirements

The insurance company maintains a central computer file on its approximately one million policies. Data are recorded on tape and on disc. The average policy is accessed approximately once every month.

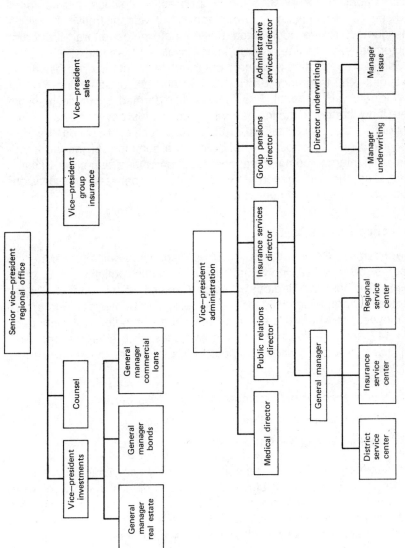

Figure 3.1 Insurance company organization.

Because of a limited time-sharing capability, the IBM 370/155 and 360/65 computers are operated principally in batch mode. They are operated 24 hours a day, 7 days a week and are staffed by 160 employees. In addition to updating the files on active policies, the computer is used for accounting, payroll, and other administrative functions. The computers are augmented by a variety of peripheral supporting equipment such as line printers, disc drives, and tape files.

The communications requirements and tasks of two representative divisions—the Insurance Service Center and the Underwriting Division—were studied in detail. The functions performed by these divisions were flowcharted to define (a) the relationships between the various sectors in the divisions, and (b) the relationships between the divisions and other groups. The following is a summary of the work task analysis, internal communications requirements, volume of transactions, and the information flow relationships between the divisions studied and the central computer.

Insurance Service Center

The Insurance Service Center (ISC) is responsible for maintaining the records on 442,229 individual life and health policies. Two other major divisions, the Regional Service Center and the District Service Center, perform essentially the same tasks. The Center consists of 178 employees, of whom 6 are executives, 25 are middle level managers, and 147 are clerical. This division averages 15.7 changes per 1000 policies in force per week. Its input to the computer is categorized as follows:

1. Optical scanner processing—24,370 entries per week.
2. Punched card input—3568 entries per week.
3. Magnetic tape—136 entries per week.

A summary of the functions performed by the Insurance Service Center is presented in Table 3.2. Figure 3.2 details the flow of work for one function: the processing of premium remittances. This table and this figure are representative of the level of detail of the analyses that were performed of the other organizational units of the company.

The ISC needs to communicate frequently with several other sectors of the company. In particular, the ISC Division contacts the following units:

1. Finance Division
The personal checks, money orders, and cash that are received as

Table 3.2. Functions Performed by Insurance Service Center

Section	Function	Level	Staff Title	Number
Change and Reinstatement	1. Changes involving kind, amounts, date, age, ratings and irregular premiums for ordinary and health policies.	7	Change Approver	7
		6	Change Examiner	8
		5	Medical Approver	1
	2. Duplicate policy transactions.	5	Assistant Examiner	9
	3. Ordinary and health reinstatements.	4	Change Coder	5
	4. Conversion of term riders & policies.	3	Reinstatement Clerk	2
	5. Insertion and removal or ordinary and heatlh policies under special remittance plans.	3	Service Clerk	4
	6. Batches input and matches computer output with source documents.	2	Change Clerk	2
	7. Reviews and attests policies and endorsements.			38
Rights and Values	1. Perform special policy calculations.	8	Calculation Approver	4
	2. Calculations of charges, allowances and commissions on ordinary and health insurance policy changes.	7	Calculation Reviewer	3
		5	Clause Clerk	3
	3. Special settlement option clauses for new issue and in force ordinary policies.	4	Assignment Clerk	3
	4. Transfer of ownership, extension of rights, and limitation of rights.	3	Clause Coder	3
	5. Records and discharge of assignments.	2	Service Clerk	2
	6. Name and beneficiary changes on ordinary policies.	4		18
	7. Batches input and matches computer output with source documents.			

Table 3.2. *Continued*

Section	Function	Level	Staff Title	Number
Commission	1. Updates commission data on computer records.	6	Computer Clerk	14
	2. Processes commission adjustments.	5	Control Clerk	2
	3. Processes credit and valuation adjustments.	3	Commission Clerk	1
	4. Replies to correspondence regarding payments.			17
	5. Controls assignments of servicing agents.			
	6. Codes the commission and valuation transactions.			
	7. Controls work into and out of the section.			
Service	1. Receives, sorts and delivers incoming mail.	5	Service Clerk	2
	2. Provides messenger service.	4	Change Typists	5
	3. Delivers keypunch briefs to keypunch area.	3	Clerk Typists	1
	4. Handles and orders all supplies.	2	Telephone Clerk	2
	5. Types policies, riders, and alteration sheets.			10
	6. Types all settlement option cases.			
	7. Types checks prepared outside of the computer			
	8. Types register cards on interoffice transfers.			
	9. Types miscellaneous letters and memos.			

Function	Tasks		Job Title	
Disbursement	1. Approves all dividend and loan transactions.	6	Disbursement Approver	4
	2. Adjusts computer master records for errors.	5	Correction Clerk	7
	3. Prepares accounting vouchers.	4	Internal Transcriber	1
	4. Controls and processes special handling items.	4	Senior Clerk	3
	5. Replies to correspondence regarding policies.	3	Service Clerk	2
				22
Billing and Remittance	1. Processes premium and policy loan.	6	Acceptance Clerk	17
	2. Controls new business remittances.	5	New Business Clerk	6
	3. Controls release of checks for over-remittance.	3	Control Clerk	9
	4. Handles voucher functions & related deposits.			
				32
Reconciliation	1. Handles requests for duplicate premium notice.	5	Service Clerk	4
	2. Investigates error conditions with remittance.	5	Reconciliation Clerk	13
	3. Investigates overdue remittances received.	3	Correction Clerk	7
	4. Handles requests to pay premium in advance.			
	5. Handles requests for return of premium paid.			
	6. Handles requests for investigations.			
	7. Processes protested checks.			24

a Transportation dependent (other than interface with postal system)

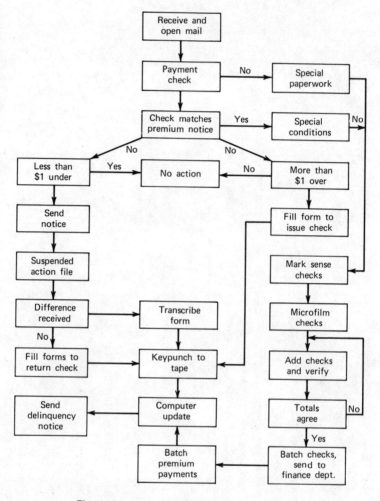

Figure 3.2 Processing of premium remittance.

payment for insurance premiums are taken to the Finance Division or to the Accounting Division; the Finance Division deposits these assets at a local bank. This occurs several times a day. This present necessity for transportation of legal tender is one of the system's constraints on telecommunications substitution, and constitutes a key issue in the banking and financial industries.

2. Computer Division

The completed data processing input forms are gathered at the end of each working day and sent to the Computer Division for processing.

3. Answer Inquiries

The ISC Division answers inquiries from insurance agents, policy-holders, and administrative insurance personnel concerning the status of a policy. The frequency varies, but generally 20 to 25 phone inquiries per day are processed.

Analysis of the flow of information within the ISC Division leads to the following conclusions:

1. ISC is a highly self-contained division. The input into the division largely consists of mail sent to pay premiums or to change information on an insurance policy. The output from the division is sent to two other divisions for further processing.

2. Speed is not a critical factor in the ISC operations. The data processing division operates on a batch mode input basis, and most large computer programs are run during off-peak hours. In addition, the need for newly updated insurance policies is not critical. A four to five day total processing time is considered adequate.

3. System security does not present a problem since the information contained in an insurance policy is not usually considered sensitive.

4. Since the computer system operates in a batch processing mode, the computer operating system does not have to be continually available for on-line interrogation. However, continuous, on-line input to a tape could replace the present process of batch keypunching changed data.

5. Any input errors to the computer can be removed during a subsequent computer processing cycle.

Underwriting Division

The primary function of the Underwriting Division is to accept or reject new applications for life and health insurance. The division consists of 6 executives, 47 middle level managers, and 47 clerical workers. Between 50,000 and 60,000 policies are issued per month.

Applications received in the life section of the Underwriting Division are placed in one of three following categories:

1. *A Cases*—No further information required for a decision.

2. *B Cases*—Only an inspection required.

3. *C Cases*—All other cases.

Sixty-five percent of the total number of applications are *A* cases and require no additional information to complete the application. *B* cases represent 20% of the total applications received. The remaining 15%, *C* cases, are more complex and require a more complete investigation.

Once an application has been evaluated and approved, the application officially becomes an insurance policy. This policy is then "issued" by entering the information into the computer system. The average policy issued has 125 characters of policy-peculiar data.

The Underwriting Division has the following contact needs (Figure 3.3):

1. Medical Department

Approximately 5% of the cases require the assistance of the Medical Department in making some of the technical judgments concerning the application. Test results must be reviewed and interpreted. Judgment must be made on the acceptability of the results. All of these contacts must be documented with written statements since the judgments must be put in the case file. The contacts are usually through interdepartmental mail.

2. Insurance Agents

Agents who have sold an application often will make a phone call or write a letter to the Underwriting Department concerning the status of that particular application. On prepaid policies, the Underwriting Department must respond within 30 days with a final decision. On other policies the Underwriting Department must respond within 45 days.

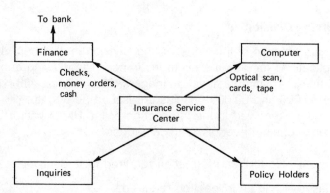

Figure 3.3   Contact requirements of the insurance service center: Finance, 3 to 5 per day; Computer, 1 per day; Inquiries; 20 to 25 per day; Mail, 1 per day.

The Underwriting Department usually receives an average of seven phone calls and three letters per day from agents.

3. Physicians
For insurance policies that require a physician's examination, contacts are always written and sent through the mail.

4. Issue Division
The Issue Division is responsible for keypunching the insurance policy into the computer system after the Underwriting Division has approved it. In the transition period (when an application becomes a policy) there are extensive information contacts between the two divisions. In addition, there are typically large amounts of physical transfer of paperwork between these two divisions.

The following conclusions can be reached about the operations of the Underwriting Division:

1. The Underwriting Division is an excellent example of an easy-to-decentralize organizational subunit within the insurance company.

2. The Underwriting Division has many contacts with other organizational subunits. However, except for the Issue Division, these are by phone or mail. Although contact with the Issue Division is currently face-to-face in many cases, the primary purpose of contact is the routine transfer of information. The physical location of the Underwriting Division or its elements is not an important factor in terms of performing the underwriting function.

Conclusions—Main Divisions

After studying the operations of both the Issue and the Underwriting Divisions, we concluded:

There is no technical need for the employees of the Issue and of the Underwriting Divisions to be collocated in a central site. Although these divisions have many contacts with other components of the insurance company, these contacts are primarily made by phone or by mail. Extensive internal communication in either division does not preclude effective dispersal through the use of telecommunications.

A second critical point was that *almost all of the routine operations of these divisions could be performed using off-the-shelf computer, terminal, and telecommunications technologies, with the communications system operating at audio bandwidths.*

These two conclusions were critical in establishing the feasibility and the design of the postulated telecommunications network. The importance of the second conclusion is elaborated upon in Chapter 5.

Satellite Offices

The insurance company presently operates two satellite offices located 20 and 25 miles from the central building with 60 and 48 employees, respectively. These satellites handle special tasks—such as group insurance health claim processing—and may be classified as being part of a fragmentation (segmentation) process, as defined in Chapter 2. The satellites were established for several reasons.

1. The central headquarters building had reached capacity.

2. The work performed at these satellites does not require frequent contact with the central headquarters.

3. They provide an opportunity for the insurance company to gain experience in managing small satellite operations.

4. They permit access to a different labor market.

5. They aid in assessing the effects of decentralization.

Newly hired workers in the satellite offices receive a reduced package of employee benefits. For example, their weekly pay is $10.00 less per employee, and they do not receive free lunches. Despite these reduced benefits, the satellites attract better-qualified personnel, as indicated in Table 3.3. This table uses 1972 data. Further, the creation

Table 3.3. Comparison of Satellite Offices and Headquarters Personnel

	Headquarters	Satellites
Ratio of number interviewed to number hired	6 to 1	1.5 to 1
Average test scores of those hired		
Arithmetic	5.4	6.0
Verbal	5.3	5.9
Average test scores of those interviewed but not hired		
Arithmetic	4.0	5.3
Verbal	4.0	4.3
First year termination rate	73%	45%
Starting salary plus benefits/week	$98	$88
Productivity	1.0	1.15

of these two satellite offices allows the insurance company to reach different labor markets. This has resulted in a reduced commuting distance for all levels of employees at the satellites.

THE BANKING INDUSTRY

In the banking industry, the other major information industry considered for detailed study, both the operational characteristics and systems requirements are radically different from the insurance company. Although banking is largely decentralized (fragmented) in its customer contacts through branches, most major banks maintain large central headquarters and data processing centers to deal with the vast amounts of paper (mostly checks) that flow daily through the branch banks. These central headquarters also provide specialized services that are in low demand at some individual branches.

In order to obtain a better understanding of the industry, the members of the research team held a series of meetings with the Director of Management Science and the Vice-President for Data Processing at one of California's largest banks. This bank handles more than one million demand deposit (checking) accounts; these accounts require updating on a daily basis.

Discussions with the bank management showed that the problems faced by the bank differ greatly from those faced by the insurance company. Although they have approximately the same number of accounts, the insurance company has an average of one transaction per account per month, whereas the bank has an average of one transaction per account per day. Errors are critical; they must be detected and corrected quickly. Security is very important to the bank, and access to the accounts must be protected. Finally, the bank requires a one-day turnaround as opposed to the three to five day turnaround considered satisfactory by most divisions of the insurance company.

The fact that the bank is not a stand-alone organization is a further complication. The paper operations of an insurance company do not depend on those of other companies; however, each bank is tied into the banking system as a whole. Thus, 45% of all checks handled by most California banks belong to a single major bank in the state. Often, only a relatively small fraction of their checks are for their own customers. The bank management expressed the opinion that there is no advantage in making improvements that would conflict with the rest of the system.

These considerations indicate that before a detailed study of the possibilities for decentralization of the paper-handling operations of banks could be achieved, an industrywide review of the banking systems' data processing and transportation operations would be necessary. Although related studies, particularly of electronic funds transfer (EFT) systems, are underway [3.2], no data telecommunications system has yet been devised that satisfies all the desired operational requirements briefly mentioned above. In order to get a clearer idea of the transportation tradeoffs, we would also have to develop information on the travel patterns to individual branches to determine whether banks hire locally or whether they generate longer distance travel comparable to that of the insurance companies. Consequently, we did not expand our research to cover this industry in greater detail.

REFERENCES

1. U.S. Department of Commerce. *Survey of Current Business, United States, 1975,* Vol. 55, No. 6. Washington, D.C.: June, 1975.
2. Anton S. Morton and Martin L. Ernst. "The Social Impacts of Electronic Funds Transfer." *IEEE Transactions on Communications,* Vol. COM–23, No. 10, October, 1975, pp. 1148–1155.

Chapter 4

Establishing Decentralization Requirements

In implementing decentralization of any organization through tele-communications, management is faced with two important decisions: (1) the number of work centers to create, and (2) the number (maximum and minimum) and types of employees to have at each work center. In an actual situation several different kinds of constraints must be satisfied when making these decisions: (1) ensuring an adequate supply of skilled labor in a particular locality; (2) meeting externally imposed constraints, such as Equal Opportunity Employment Guidelines; (3) meeting corporate and government policy restrictions; and (4) designing the optimum task accomplishment system to ensure maintenance or improvement of labor productivity. In meeting these constraints a company will usually try to minimize net costs as its overall corporate goal. Typical costs to be considered are those of telecommunications equipment, transportation, office overhead, rental and maintenance, and inefficiency of operation.

An optimization model was developed (Figure 4.1) as a means for analyzing the tradeoffs involved in making a telecommunications-transportation substitution. This model is sufficiently general so that it can be applied to any information industry firm. It serves as the framework in assessing the economic feasibility of substituting telecommunications for physical transportation,.and helps to define the functional requirements for an optimal operating network.

The model consists of five interrelated submodels. Each of the submodels represents a constraint on, or a component of, the general model. For example, detailed element lists of the regional data and contact requirements submodels are shown in Tables 4.1 and 4.2. Figure 4.2 shows the interrelationships of the submodels, and Figure 4.3

35

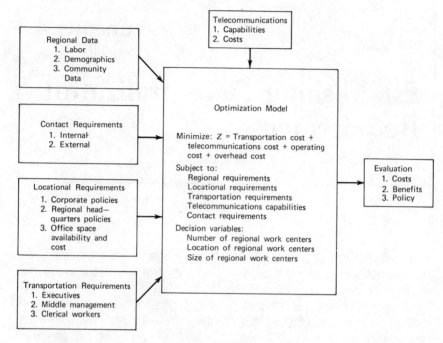

Figure 4.1   Generalized transportation/telecommunications tradeoff model.

shows the relationships between the parameters of the model.

The basic concept of dispersion of a firm (as defined in Chapter 2) and its implications for transportation and communication can be illustrated by Figure 4.4. The hypothetical example under consideration is a major information industry organization that is located in a single, central building. The firm is a heavy user of data processing equipment and a large percentage of the employees are directly involved with clerical tasks. From a transportation viewpoint, the operation of the firm is depicted in Figure 4.4. The geographical area from which the company draws its employees has been divided into 16 approximately equal segments identified by numbers 1 through 16. The headquarters of the firm is typically in the central business district of a major metropolitan area. If the firm were to disperse its operations into four satellite offices, as shown in Figure 4.4*b*, the distance traveled by the employees would be considerably reduced. The only employees who would continue to report to the central headquarters and who would live at greater-than-usual distances from it would be some high-level executives and some specialized support services such as the Legal Department. These employees usually constitute only a small percentage of the total employee work force.

Table 4.1. Detailed Element List

I. Labor Availability
   A. High schools and other educational institutions
      1. Number
      2. Enrollment
      3. Training provided
   B. Total office employment of region
      1. Insurance companies
      2. Banks
      3. Financial institutions
      4. Government agencies
   C. Labor history
      1. Extent of unionization
      2. Industries unionized
II. Demographics
   A. Income distribution
   B. Education
   C. Housing and rental
      1. Availability
      2. Cost
      3. Location
   D. Age of population
   E. Ethnic compositions
      1. Black
      2. Spanish surname
      3. White
      4. Other
III. Community Data
   A. Police
      1. Personnel
      2. Equipment
      3. Incidents of crime
   B. Fire
      1. Personnel
      2. Equipment
      3. Incidence
   C. Physical facilities
      1. Streets and highways
      2. Sewers
      3. Hospitals
   D. Taxes
      1. Rates
      2. Assessments
   E. Public transit
      1. Availability
      2. Cost
      3. Convenience

Table 4.2. Detailed Element List of Contact Requirements Submodel

I. Contact paths definition
  A. Within an organizational unit
  B. Between organizational units
  C. External to the company or organization
II. Contact content modality and traffic
  A. Purpose of contact
    1. Face-to-face
    2. Telephone
    3. Letter/paperwork
    4. Computer
    5. Teleprinter
  B. Frequency of contact required
    1. Face-to-face
    2. Telephone
    3. Letter/paperwork
    4. Computer
    5. Teleprinter
  C. Amount of information required of contact
    1. Face-to-face
    2. Telephone
    3. Letter/paperwork
    4. Computer
    5. Teleprinter

It should be noted that Figure 4.4b illustrates a dispersed network, that is, each employee would report to the center nearest his home, regardless of his rank or function. A fragmented network, in which the centers are specialized, could easily result in an increase in transportation if workers had to travel to a center at some arbitrary distance from their homes in order to perform their work (although this is currently the most common case of decentralization found in the United States). This is shown in Figure 4.4c.

Given these general considerations the specific locations of the satellite offices, the number of offices, and the geographical areas assigned to supply the labor pool for the offices must now be determined. It is at this point that other cost considerations and company constraints become important.

COST CONSIDERATIONS

The creation of satellite office locations influences a number of costs, primarily transportation, telecommunications, operating, and overhead

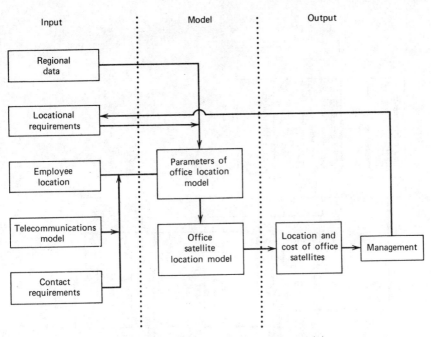

Figure 4.2   Schematic diagram of the model.

costs. Transportation costs should decrease as more dispersed satellite offices are established. Transportation costs are a product of the average distance traveled per employee, the number of employees, and the cost per mile to commute. With the creation of additional office satellites, the transportation costs decrease, since the average distance traveled to work decreases (assuming that workers go to the nearest satellite).

Telecommunications costs should increase as more satellite offices are established, primarily because functions once performed by means of other, possibly less expensive modes of communication (such as face-to-face conversations), now require telecommunication. However, the marginal cost of telecommunications operations is relatively insensitive to the number of satellite operations. Telecommunications costs include the costs of hardware, software, and data transmission. As more satellite offices are created the telecommunications costs rise to the extent that some additional hardware must be provided at each site. Software, since it is generally systemwide in its application, is relatively unaffected by the number of satellites. The key factor in most of these cost elements is that there must be enough employees at a given satellite location to warrant the use of the necessary data

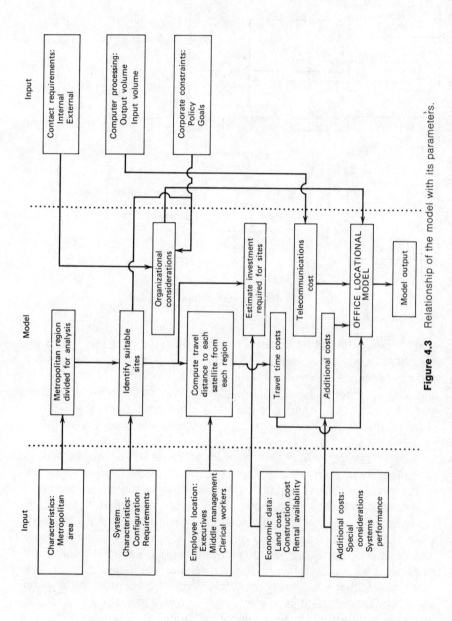

Figure 4.3 Relationship of the model with its parameters.

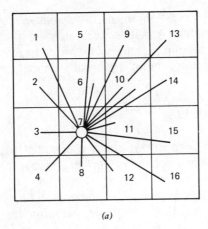

(a)

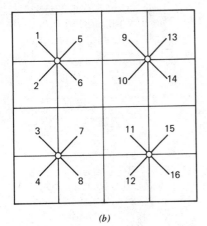

(b)

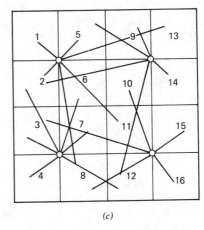

(c)

Figure 4.4 Impact of firm dispersion on transportation: (a) one central headquarters; (b) four satellite offices and one central headquarters—Dispersed; (c) four satellite offices and one central headquarters—Fragmented.

concentrators and associated wideband data lines that make the telecommunications system most effective.

The office overhead costs are variable, depending on the circumstances of each case. Based on the insurance company's experience with its satellite offices, it appears that employee turnover and training costs decrease, along with salary costs and office space costs. Higher productivity at the satellite offices also lowers overhead costs. Additional office equipment and office machines and a higher inventory of supplies at the centers can result in increased costs (i.e., reduced pooling of materials and supplies, plus an inventory level requirement at each center that might be slightly higher than the equivalent for the same number of employees at a central location).

CASE STUDY MODEL

As a preliminary step in designing a specific dispersion model for the insurance company subject of our case study, reference was made to the Los Angeles Basin Planning Document [4.1]. This document, compiled for the Los Angeles Department of City Planning, projects trends and recommends development patterns for the Los Angeles Basin to 1990.

One of the key recommendations of the Planning Document was the development of 35 regional centers throughout the Los Angeles Basin and the San Fernando Valley (Table 4.3). The team used the locations of these 35 planned regional centers as potential sites for remote work

Table 4.3. Thirty-five Regional Centers

Central Area	San Fernando Valley
1. Boyle Heights	19. Canoga Park[a]
2. Central City[a]	20. Chatsworth
3. Hollywood[a]	21. Encino[a]
4. North and East Century City	22. Granada Hills
5. Northeast Los Angeles[a]	23. Mission Hills
6. South Central Los Angeles	24. North Hollywood
7. Silver Lake	25. Northridge[a]
8. Southeast Los Angeles[a]	26. Pacoima[a]
9. West Adams[a]	27. Reseda
10. Westlake	28. Sherman Oaks[a]
11. Wilshire[a]	29. Sunland
	30. Sylmar[a]
Western Area	31. Van Nuys
12. Bel Air	32. Verdugo[a]
13. Brentwood	
14. Palms[a]	*Southern Area*
15. Venice	32. San Pedro[a]
16. Westchester[a]	33. Torrance[a]
17. Westwood	35. Wilmington
18. West Los Angeles[a]	

[a] Eighteen centers selected from set.

centers. We then performed an analysis of the commuting distance for each of the company's employees to the center nearest his or her home. The insurance company provided employee residence location data by ZIP code. The employee residences were assumed to be uni-

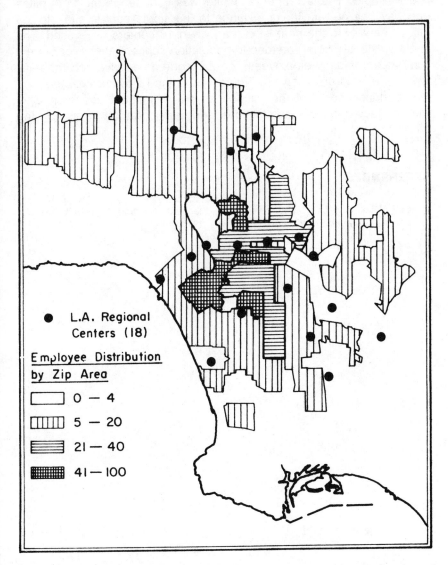

Figure 4.5 Residential distribution of insurance company employees (number of employees residing in each zip code area). Locations of 18 urban centers specified by the Los Angeles City General Plan.

formly distributed within any zip area. The centroids of the employee zip code areas were used to compute the travel distances to the headquarters. The most feasible 18 centers were then selected from the original 35 (locations noted in Table 4.3) in order to provide a baseline example. The average commute was reduced from 10.7 miles one way (the current travel distance to the single central site), to 3.9 miles one way to the nearest center, when 18 centers were used. The centers selected corresponded to population concentrations for current insurance company employees; the ZIP code areas in which the centers are located are shown in Figure 4.5. In the following chapters, the transportation costs of the employees are calculated and compared with projected telecommunications and transportation costs for the 18 centers selected.

REFERENCES

1. City of Los Angeles, Department of City Planning. *Planning Area 1990: Population, Housing and Employment Projections*, 1974.

Chapter 5

General Telecommunications Network Considerations

The main objective of this portion of the research was to determine the technological and cost feasibility of implementing a telecommuting system in place of the common hub-oriented transportation system. In order to gain some perspective on telecommunications policy issues, we considered both private and public networks. The commuting distances of the personnel at the insurance company and the general information requirements of the company were used to formulate a hypothetical network configuration. Several sets of alternative requirements were postulated to determine cost impacts. An analysis was made of the human factors involved in the design of a telecommunications network of the type envisioned and, as part of this analysis, a series of scenarios were developed to illustrate the relationships between the human factors and technological requirements of alternative networks. In all cases, the costs of the network were estimated conservatively.

The hypothetical network configuration was based on the establishment of 18 regional centers such as those discussed in Chapter 4. These centers are now, or are proposed to be, major areas of population and/or commerce within the Los Angeles Basin; they constitute the basis for a baseline estimate of the practical possibilities for near term dispersion. Since the insurance company's central office is located near the central business district of Los Angeles, a simple star communications network would suffice to serve the regional centers. The postulated network radiates from the site in or near the present corporate offices where the main computing system would be located.

In calculating the costs of the network, it was assumed that the cost of acquiring the remote site real estate and facilities would be less than, or at most equal to, costs of maintaining the downtown facility of 2500 employees. This assumption is based on the premise that the costs of construction would be offset by the appreciated value of the real estate in central Los Angeles and on the fact that office space in the central business district currently sells for a high premium cost relative to the average costs of real estate at the regional center locations (see Chapter 8). Further, it was assumed that the building or rental costs of the remote facilities would not be significantly increased by the installation of terminals and remote computing equipment and the increased loads on air conditioning and other facilities. Our experience with the design of buildings that house computerized office environments, such as the Information Sciences Institute at the University of Southern California, leads us to believe that this is a reasonable assumption.

Another critical assumption is that the data rates (which we have estimated from data rates associated with the current computing rates at the insurance company) would not increase by an order of magnitude. Currently, the insurance company processes a very large amount of data utilizing computer equipment. This processing does not represent the entire work load for every employee within the insurance company. However, it does represent a significant portion of the volume of work accomplished by the clerical personnel who would be dispersed. It is clear that there would be an increased load on the telecommunications system as a result of additional interoffice memoranda and other associated managerial tasks such as monitoring of clerical personnel through the telecommunications system.

The network design for a "worst case" (i.e., the most expensive option) would involve the allocation of a terminal to every dispersed employee. Our analysis of the insurance company information flow leads us to believe that present computer usage requirements could be satisfied by one terminal for every 5 to 30 employees, depending on the particular work pattern. If the system does not allocate one terminal per employee there is a further need to account for queuing problems. Queuing is essentially a function of terminal use, that is, if there is less than one terminal per employee at each site, then some period of time conceivably could be spent by employees waiting for terminals to become available. The queuing problem cannot be answered explicitly without knowledge of the mean arrival time of employees requesting service at terminals. We have not yet gathered information to this level of detail; however, it is reasonable to expect that no significant queuing would occur with one terminal per five employees.

A final assumption was made that an audio bandwidth system would be used. This assumption was based on analysis of the functions of the Issue and the Underwriting Divisions of the insurance company (see Chapter 3). This analysis indicated that the functions of these divisions could be performed at remote locations using an audio bandwidth telecommunications system. This point is critical, since a network designed for audio bandwidths influences other features of the system and means, among other things, that a user-specific system is unnecessary. This latter point is also particularly important since it permits a wider applicability of the research findings.

PRIVATE NETWORK

Before discussing the costs of the private network it is necessary to review the basic design and cost assumptions. As indicated in Chapter 4, 18 regional centers were selected. In our hypothetical network design site 2 (Table 4.3) would be the central site and, as such, would house the main computer. This site would be located 0.3 mile from the current central site. This number is not critical and was picked only because of the further assumption that the company would move the center to another nearby building when it dispersed.

Assumptions

The 18 centers provide a reasonable reduction of commuting distance for the insurance company employees without increasing the costs of the telecommunications network beyond reasonable limits. The primary cost assumption for the private network was that each center would be linked with the main computation center via a coaxial cable installation. A coaxial cable installation was chosen because of the ability to have a major expansion in data volume without requiring new transmission lines. Given the assumption that the centers would be hard-wired to the computer in the focal location, it was necessary to estimate the installation costs of the cable. This task was difficult since the costs associated with the installation of coaxial cable vary considerably. Depending on where and how the cable is installed, the cost can be as high as $1 million per mile.

The variance in installation costs is partly due to different local ordinances prohibiting exposed wiring. In these cases there is a consequent cost of digging up streets. Lower costs per mile are possible in those areas where it is possible to use above ground installation techniques such as the common "telephone pole" installation. For example, to trench down Fifth Avenue in midtown Manhattan, if it could be done at all, would be considerably more expensive than stringing cable on telephone poles through a residential area. It is important to note that, except in those areas where installation costs would be extremely high, the cable installation represents a relatively small portion of the total cost. For example, the total length of inter-center cable in our hypothetical network was 205 miles. At $3000 per mile (the estimated average installation cost for our network), the installation cost would be $615,000, or 9% of the total network cost. Even these percentages give distorted pictures of the relative costs since the proposed cable network would have a data capacity far in excess of that used for estimating the other costs.

To add this other dimension to the installation cost, it should be noted that if the maximum number of employees in a single center is, for example, 230, and even if only one strand of coaxial cable is pulled to each center, then a significantly higher bandwidth for data transmission is available than is necessary. Assume, for the 230 employee case, that each terminal were operated at 2400 baud (i.e., 240 characters per second). With one terminal per employee, one voice grade line per terminal would be required. If a 260 megahertz bandwidth is assumed for the coaxial cable, then approximately 30,000 to 45,000 two-way 2400 baud lines could be multiplexed into it (assuming no other use of the cable). This is a factor of 200 greater than the number of employees at even the largest center in our hypothetical network and assumes only that contemporary telephone technology is used.

The $3000 per mile cost mentioned above for our hypothetical network represents the estimated average cost of installing coaxial cable in the Los Angeles area; the figure was determined through discussion with several cable television consultants and includes allowances for incremental installation. Incremental installation means that costs are shared between the installer of the cable and one or more public utilities. For example, when the cable must be buried a trench of 6 feet or more would be dug down the center of the road. Of this, 5 feet of the trench would belong to the public utilities (e.g., power, sewer, gas, and water), and 1 foot would belong to the installer of the cable.

There is a fixed cost at each center associated with the installation of the telecommunications system. That fixed cost includes the cost of a high-speed line printer, an input-output controller or multiplexer, and additional space and power requirements. If we assume that each center uses a fairly sophisticated high-speed line printer, the fixed cost per center would be approximately $120,000. A line printer was included for each center on the assumption that hard copies (i.e., printed on paper) of data files would be needed from the central computer location. The actual need for hard copies would be dependent on the data needs of the employees at each center. To determine these needs in detail, it would be necessary to know: (a) the dispersion of employees, broken down by work function, to the 18 centers; and (b) the need for each work function at each center for hard copies of the central data files. Lacking this information, a simple assumption was to include one high-speed printer per center. While this is again a "worst case" analysis, it is also reasonable to expect that larger centers might require several line printers while other locations might not require any.

The cost of the terminal was estimated at several levels, primarily to show the impact of the terminal cost upon the total network cost. The simplest terminal would be the Teletype variety, with an approximate purchase price of $1100, although significant reductions in cost presumably would be possible with bulk purchasing. The most expensive terminal, which would cost approximately $5000, would be a sophisticated, "intelligent" printing terminal, with on-line editing and formatting capabilities. Some CRT terminals are now available for about $2500 which also have fairly extensive formatting capabilities. A mix of terminals would be most probable with the mix being designed to specifically meet the needs of the employees at each site. It is quite possible, judging from the experience of USC's Information Sciences Institute, that a large number of these would be CRT terminals, that is, with a television-type display, rather than a printed output. This step would eliminate a large fraction of actual paperwork. Cost savings from these paperless transactions are not included in these estimates.

In summary, the cost of installation of coaxial cable is estimated at $3000 per mile. The fixed cost per center is approximately $120,000. The cost per employee is essentially the cost of the terminal and its maintenance divided by the number of employees per terminal. There is a small facilities increase associated with wiring each work station for terminal access, but it is assumed that this cost would be absorbed in construction or rental of the facility.

Hypothetical Private Networks

The 18 centers produce the dispersed network design shown schematically in Figure 5.1, with the computer housed at the central site. To illustrate some of the configuration alternatives, five hypothetical cases are presented for the 18-center configuration and one hypothetical case is given for a 35-center configuration. The section con-

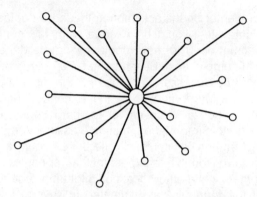

Figure 5.1 Eighteen-Center network design.

cludes with an 18-center configuration and network design that assumes fewer terminals and calculates capital and maintenance costs as they would be incurred by the insurance company studied. In cases I, II, III, and VII, the following assumptions were made:

1.   The 18 centers are the same size and location in each case.

2.   The fixed cost per center is $120,000.

3.   The installation cost of the coaxial cable is $3000 per mile.

4.   The total number of miles in the network is 205.

5.   The cost of paper associated with the computer terminals is approximately the same as the cost of paper used by the employees now, i.e., there is no marginal cost or savings.

6.   Hard copy would be available through the line printer at each center.

7.   One terminal per employee would be provided for the 2048 employees who hold clerical and middle management positions.

8.   All equipment is purchased by the company.

9.   The basic capital costs do not include amortization or maintenance charges.

10.   Only the marginal costs are to be considered, that is, the cost of the central computer is not included, nor is special software development included because of the relatively simple types of data transmission contemplated.

11.   Insurance and property tax costs are not included.

The variable factor in the first three cases is the cost per employee, that is, the cost of the terminal.

In Case I the terminal cost is set at an average of $2000, which would bring the total network cost to approximately $6,872,000. This price terminal would allow automatic form display, for example, where the employee would only be required to "fill in" the blanks pointed out by the terminal. In Case II the network cost is reduced to $5,029,-000 by postulating a cheaper, "dumb" terminal that would cost $1100. Case III is based on an assumed terminal cost of $5000, representing a highly sophisticated terminal. Use of the more expensive terminal would bring the total network cost to approximately $13,016,000. Cases I through III are summarized in Table 5.1. It is clear, from these cases, that the principal factor in the total costs of the hypothetical. network is the number and the type of terminals used by the employees, at least in cases of high terminal population.

In Case IV (Table 5.2) an alternate selection of 18 centers was made, which changed the total network miles slightly. However, the other assumptions given for Cases I through III remain the same. The average cost of $2000 per terminal was again used as a basis for calculation. The network cost in Case IV was approximately $6,868,000 (as compared to $6,872,000 for Case I), indicating that the cost of the network is relatively insensitive to the details of the location of the centers, assuming that the selection is at all "reasonable."

Although in Los Angeles and in most urban areas in the United States point-to-point microwave channels are already crowding the available broadcast spectrum, the possibilities of microwave or optical point-to-point links were explored for comparison purposes. In Case V the assumption was made that an infrared communications link, rather than cable, would be established between the original 18 centers. The infrared link used (assuming "off-the-shelf" technology) does not, with present commercial technology, have the cable's capacity of 260 million bits per second, but it could easily have a capacity in the order of 100 kilobit per second (kbps). A bandwidth of 100 kbps would still support data transmission by approximately 35 employees, based on a rate of 2400 baud (20% guard bands). With a terminal mix that used a significant number of terminals that were "only" capable of operating at 30 characters per second, the number of employees that could be supported would increase by a factor 8. Note that 30 characters per second is the equivalent of 300 words (or one double-spaced page) per minute for normal text trans-

Table 5.1.   Network Costs for Cases I, II, and III

Node	Miles from Central	Number of Employees at Node	Cost of Node ($) (Case I)	Cost of Node ($) (Case II)	Cost of Node ($) (Case III)
1	0.3	230	$581,000	$374,000	$1,271,000
2	11	114	382,000	279,000	724,000
3	7	59	259,000	206,000	436,000
4	4	128	387,000	271,000	771,000
5	4	121	373,000	164,000	736,000
6	7	129	399,000	283,000	786,000
7	4	211	553,000	363,000	1,186,000
8	13	214	587,000	395,000	1,229,000
9	23	102	394,000	302,000	700,000
10	11	64	281,000	224,000	473,000
11	17	46	265,000	224,000	403,000
12	4	109	350,000	252,000	677,000
13	8	197	539,000	362,000	1,130,000
14	11	118	388,000	282,000	742,000
15	17	63	298,000	241,000	487,000
16	21	63	310,000	253,000	499,000
17	20	25	229,000	207,000	304,000
18	22	55	297,000	248,000	462,000

Cost per center: $120,000
Coaxial cable installation cost/mile: $3000
Number of employees: 2048
Terminal cost (one per employee):
  Case I: $2000
  Case II: $1100
  Case III: $5000
Total capital cost of network:
  Case I: $6,872,000
  Case II: $5,029,00
  Case III: $13,016,000
Average commuting distance (round trip): 7 miles

mission. This would yield a maximum number of employees per center of approximately 280, or 50 more employees than the largest center postulated.

Instead of using a cable cost factor, as in the previous cases, we increased the cost per center by $120,000, postulating the use of the infrared point-to-point links for center interconnect. Other network

Table 5.2. Network Costs for Case IV (18 Different Sites)

Node	Miles from Central Node	Number of Employees at Node	Cost of Node ($) (Case IV)
1	12	62	$280,000
2	8	49	241,000
3	3	326	782,000
4	13	120	399,000
5	10	179	507,000
6	6	72	383,000
7	13	97	352,000
8	5	256	447,000
9	3	202	532,000
10	4	171	475,000
11	11	106	365,000
12	11	47	246,000
13	7	88	317,000
14	28	39	281,000
15	27	19	240,000
16	10	118	386,000
17	19	59	296,000
18	15	138	440,000

Cost per center: $120,000
Coaxial cable installation cost/mile: $3000
Number of employees: 2048
Terminal cost (one per employee): $2000
Total cost of network: $6,868,000
Average commuting distance (round trip): 6.8 miles

assumptions remain the same. This cost-per-center estimate is open to question because, if many centers were to be so equipped, then it would only be possible (because of spectrum crowding problems) to design point-to-point communications systems based on modulated signals transmitted at or near the frequency of light. In Los Angeles where dense fog and smog are frequent enough to be a consideration, repeater stations would be required on the longest point-to-point communications links. Nevertheless, we felt that $240,000 per center was approximately correct. It was interesting to note that the cost of the network, compared to Case I, increased by approximately $1.6 million (Table 5.3). It should also be noted that with the probable advent of low cost optical fiber transmission systems in the next decade,

Table 5.3.   Network Costs for Case V (Infrared Communication Link)

Node	Miles from Central Node	Number of Employees at Node	Cost of Node ($) (Case IV)
1	11	114	$468,000
2	7	59	358,000
3	4	128	496,000
4	0.3	230	700,000
5	4	121	482,000
6	7	129	498,000
7	4	211	662,000
8	13	214	668,000
9	23	102	444,000
10	11	64	368,000
11	18	46	332,000
12	3	109	458,000
13	8	197	634,000
14	11	118	476,000
15	17	63	366,000
16	21	63	366,000
17	20	25	290,000
18	22	55	350,000

Cost per center: $240,000
Cost per mile: $0.0
Number of employees: 2048
Terminal cost (one per employee): $2000
Total cost of network: $8,416,000
Average commuting distance (round trip): 7 miles

enormous gains in bandwidth capability between centers will be possible at essentially the same cost of installation as a cable system. Hence, the point-to-point system does not appear to be very attractive.

Case VI (Table 5.4) is a recalculation of Case I using the 35 centers of the Los Angeles Planning Document instead of the 18 centers used in the previous cases. The cost and design assumptions are the same as those given for Case I. The approximate cost of a 35-center network would be $9,736,000, an increase of approximately $3 million over Case I, although the average employee round trip commute distance would decrease by only 1.4 miles with the addition of 17 centers. This observation indicates that the decrease in commuting miles beyond the 18-center baseline case, although representing an annual cost saving to each employee of about $50 (an annual total for

Table 5.4. Network Costs for 35 Centers (Case VI)

Node	Miles from Central Node	Number of Employees at Node	Cost of Node ($) (Case IV)
1	12	61	$278,000
2	8	35	213,000
3	3	326	782,000
4	9	15	176,000
5	13	101	361,000
6	10	135	419,000
7	6	56	251,000
8	13	55	268,000
9	5	156	447,000
10	5	15	166,000
11	3	202	532,000
12	7	0	142,000
13	11	12	176,000
14	4	171	475,000
15	11	106	365,000
16	11	38	228,000
17	7	11	164,000
18	7	65	271,000
19	28	39	281,000
20	27	10	222,000
21	15	17	198,000
22	24	9	210,000
23	19	16	209,000
24	10	88	326,000
25	22	8	201,000
26	18	13	201,000
27	19	34	246,000
28	7	33	208,000
29	18	9	191,000
30	22	5	197,000
31	14	81	326,000
32	17	31	234,000
33	29	5	216,000
34	19	69	315,000
35	27	21	242,000

Cost per center: $120,000
Coaxial cable installation cost per mile: $3000
Number of employees: 2048
Terminal cost (one per employee): $2000
Total cost of network: $9,736,000
Average commuting distance (round trip): 5.6 miles

employees of $125,000) would not justify the increase in either administrative or capital costs of the larger telecommunications network.

In Case VII, we reduced the size of the group of employees who would be working with terminals to the 1800 clerical workers and attempted to calculate the costs as they might actually be incurred by the insurance company. Thus, rather than assume a one-time cost, we amortized the cost to the insurance company over a 10-year period at 10% interest. However, since amortization is frequently done over a five-year or shorter period by the computer industry, calculations were also done for a five-year amortization period. A "worst case" situation was assumed, with no resale value being allowed at the end of the amortization period. A moderately high terminal cost of $2500 was assumed, allowing for a fairly sophisticated terminal such as the automatic form-setting type mentioned earlier. The same installation and center costs were assumed for the baseline 18-center case.

Three alternative terminal investments were calculated. In option A, a total of 1800 terminals was assumed (one for each clerical employee) for a total terminal cost of $4,500,000. In option B, two employees per terminal were assumed (900 terminals at $2500 each) for a total terminal cost of $2,250,000. Five clerical workers per terminal were assumed in option C, for a total of 360 terminals costing $900,000.

The annual amortized capital cost per employee for each of the three terminal options was calculated, for both the 5- and 10-year amortization periods. The annual system maintenance costs per employee were also estimated using a base rate of $20 per month for each terminal. Finally, the gross annual network cost per employee was calculated for the total insurance company population of 2500, again considering the three terminal options over the two amortization periods.

The summary of this analysis is presented in Table 5.5. These calculations indicate that the average annual cost per employee would range between $275 and $935, depending on the assumptions used. Although the dollar and energy costs of telecommuting, as compared to commuting, are discussed in more detail in Chapter 6, some initial observations may be made. First, commuting costs probably will continue to rise as the costs of materials, labor, and gasoline continue to contribute to rising costs of automobile production and operation. Purchase costs of telecommunications and computer equipment, on the other hand, may be expected to decrease slightly as sales volumes continue to increase and the technologies improve. Operation

Table 5.5.   Dispersed Telecommuting Network Costs with Maintenance, Amortization

---

Assumptions:
 Number of nodes: 18
 Average commuting distance (round trip):
  Current (single central location): 21.4 miles
  Dispersed: 7.0 miles
Fixed investment for private network installation: $2,775,000
 Interface computer hardware (at $120,000/node): $2,160,000
 Internodal cable installation (at $3000/mile): $615,000
Variable investment for computer terminals (at $2500 each):
 A. 1800 terminals (one per clerical employee): $4,500,000
 B. 900 terminals (two clerical workers per terminal): $2,250,000
 C. 360 terminals (five clerical workers per terminal): $900,000
Annual amortized capital cost per employee:[a]

5-Year Amortization	10-Year Amortization
A. $770	A. $470
B. $530	B. $330
C. $390	C. $240

Annual system maintenance costs per employee (est.)
A.	$170
B.	$ 85
C.	$ 35

Gross annual network cost per employee:[a]

5-Year Amortization	10-Year Amortization
A. $935	A. $640
B. $615	B. $410
C. $425	C. $275

---

[a] Equal amount payment method, 10% interest, 2500 employees, rounded to nearest $5. Costs are exclusive of insurance and property taxes on the hardware.

costs, of course, can be expected to rise for both automobiles and communications equipment as energy continues to become scarcer and more valuable. However, since the operating energy consumption of telecommunications hardware is considerably lower than that of transportation system, the impact on telecommuting of those higher prices will not be as significant, and will become less so as alternative sources to fossil fuels for electrical energy are developed.

COMMON CARRIER NETWORK

The cost of using a common carrier network was estimated as an alternative to a private network. The primary points of interest were: (a) the cost to the insurance company of leasing lines from a public utility, as opposed to the cost of private cable installation, and (b) the capability of the public network.

The baseline assumptions were the same as for the private network: 18 centers, a central computer, a terminal cost of $2000, and a center cost of $120,000.

The leasing costs that would be incurred by the company were based on standard rate charges associated with a telephone utility in Los Angeles. An initial estimate was made based on the costs of voice grade, full duplex lines interconnecting each terminal in the centers with the central computer. This cost was prohibitive and was discarded.

A second estimate was based on the installation of two 50-kbit lines to each of the centers using a "message concentrator," that is, a minicomputer with appropriate data storage capacity, to convert the local terminal message traffic to the equivalent of twenty, full duplex 2400-baud lines multiplexed on two 50-kbit transmission lines. The installation of the pairs of 50-kbit lines to the centers would require a one-time charge of $35,000. The annual lease charges for the lines used would be approximately $409,000. The leased line charge is more expensive when compared to the amortized costs of the coaxial cable installation. The annual payment for coaxial cable installation, amortized over a 10-year period at 10% interest, would be $100,000. Over a five-year amortization period, the annual payment would be $162,000 and, by the end of the amortization period, the cable would be owned by the company.

The leased line would have a much lower bandwidth, offering only a 100-kbit capacity as opposed to the 260-kbit capability that would be possible with the coaxial cable. Also, it should be noted that the higher bandwidth capacity of the private network raises the possibility of cost sharing with other dispersed companies.

However, the common carrier network does offer some advantages to the insurance company. The leased line would not tie the company to a long-term investment, especially during a period of rapid technological change in the communications field. Also, under the lease agreement with the public utility the company would not incur additional maintenance, insurance, or property tax charges, whereas such charges are probable with the private network. Finally, the private network as configured here (i.e., in a star pattern) lacks the path diversity and innately higher system reliability of the common carrier network. Diversifying the network would increase its cost somewhat. On the basis of all these considerations it must be concluded that the common carrier public utility network represents a viable alternative to a private network using coaxial cable.

Chapter 6

Some Human Factor Considerations and Operating Scenarios

The ability of workers to interact successfully with telecommunications equipment is largely a human factors concern. Unfortunately very little research has been done on the human factors involved in the use of such technology by clerical workers; most studies are directed toward managerial use of telecommunication [6.1–6.3]. This chapter discusses some of the human factors that should be considered in the use of telecommunications by clerical workers.

CLERICAL WORKERS

Job Satisfaction and Turnover

One major consideration that can seriously affect costs and productivity in information industries is job satisfaction and turnover. The reasons behind a given level of job satisfaction are a composite of human factors variables: relative anxiety, depression, ability to perform assigned tasks, the presence of friends, perceived antagonisms, pleasant working conditions, and so on. The impacts of the workers' feelings, attitudes, and perceptions, both on the individual and on the group level, are difficult to assess, as they are only partially reflected in productivity and in job turnover. The impact of a telecommunications system on the work environment, and the importance of this impact, have never been clearly demonstrated. However some related studies, albeit informal ones, have isolated some of the effects that must be anticipated and measured by an organization that is contemplating changeover to a telecommunications mode.

In two major East Coast financial institutions where interviews were held during our research, personnel were transferred from manual methods of coding to limited computer communications systems (primarily input). Preliminary case data suggest that as a result of this transfer there was a decline in group morale, an increase in the release and transfer of older personnel, and a high turnover among young personnel. The following four major factors were isolated:

1. Asking employees to travel to the central organization to perform routine tasks on a machine quickly alienated them.

2. To alleviate the decline in morale and to keep turnover rates acceptable, significantly higher monetary incentives were necessary.

3. Older employees, who tended to rely more heavily on interpersonal demonstrations of productivity, were intimidated by the computers which made objective measurements of their output.

4. Some older, clerical level employees were unable to adapt to man–machine relationships and had to be transferred.

To counteract this negative impression it is interesting to note that, in the case of the insurance company we studied, the employees who were trained in the use of CRT terminals prior to transfer to the satellite offices (see Chapter 3), have evinced a high level of enthusiasm for working in this new mode. In fact, the company has encountered the problem of a "status symbol" effect, that is, workers whose work loads do not justify the expense of a terminal for their sole use are also requesting terminals, presumably on the basis of a high level of positive response and motivation exhibited by their fellow employees.

The disparity between the employee attitudes in the first and the second instances suggests that training, organizational attitudes, and orientation may be critical factors in system design. Certainly the initial baseline measurements should be carefully designed to determine the possible presence of negative attitudes. The system design and implementation should then be modified to counter such attitudes.

This observation may be further supported by the experience of the USC Information Sciences Institute (ISI). At ISI clerical employees are trained to use CRT terminals and learn to interact with the ARPA/ TENEX system. The ARPANET is a complex system of geographically widespread computer facilities interconnected by telecommunications. TENEX is the operating software system for the network. Computer-naive staff are trained at ISI under the supervision of sophisticated computer science personnel over a period of approximately six months in an on-the-job training atmosphere. The learning atmosphere is very positive since organizational norms are highly supportive of computer terminal communications. Consequently ISI has experienced a relatively low turnover rate and a high morale among the clerical personnel.

User Acceptability of the Man–Machine Interface

User acceptability of the CRT or Teletype terminal in central data base communications is also dependent on software support. Software support determines the ease with which stored data are found and the way in which they are represented in display. Acceptability will be affected by the software type and format of information the support generates during turnaround interludes, and by the degree of closure or feedback it offers users in confirming acceptance of their inputs.

Languages used in the computer network can vary in their similarity to natural languages. Hence the degree of training users must have to understand and use them will also vary. The extent to which the languages are "natural" (through training or similarity to English) will affect acceptability. The extent to which the user understands the workings of the network itself will also affect acceptability.

The physical configuration of the terminals, their accessibility to the central and local data bases, the extent to which the terminals can work effectively off-line, and the availability of terminals and user information services are all relevant factors in the work environment in terms of their effects on user acceptability.

SCENARIOS

Overview

To obtain a better understanding of both human factors and technological requirements for the postulated network, a series of scenarios were developed by the research team. The scenarios are summarized in this section, and the technological requirements for each system postulated are noted in Figure 6.1. They are intended to explore and

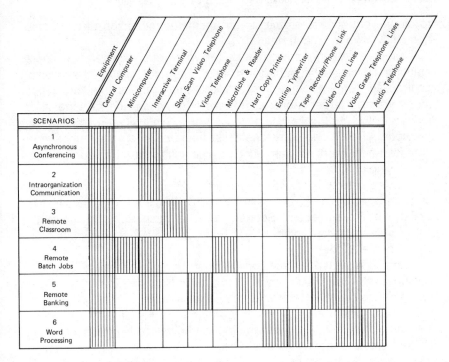

Figure 6.1   Technological requirements for scenarios.

to illustrate some of the possibilities for telecommuting rather than to provide an exhaustive directory of them.

The scenarios envision workers in various telecommunications environments. The first scenario (1A), on asynchronous managerial conferencing, pictures the use of CRT terminals to interface ongoing communications with fellow members of a conference group. The messages are stored in a central computer facility. This system could be described as a dedicated electronic mail system, "dedicated" in the sense that access to the system is private.

Scenario 1B attempts to illustrate the problems of the naive user of a system in which a command language is needed for access to information. The system described is location-independent in the sense that as long as the conferee has access to a computer terminal and a telephone link, he has access to the conference. It is time-independent in the sense that messages can be read from storage or can be written into storage at any time. However the system may present access problems requiring support facilities for their solution. Training of users, software support, and support personnel are possible ways to circumvent access problems; an optimal combination of such solutions may have to be determined.

In lieu of training many users to work with terminals or implementing an extensive support system, Scenario 2 suggests training centralized terminal operators (telecommunications mediators) for members of a larger group to retrieve information and to send information to the central computer facility or to similar operators in other divisions. Such a secretary–specialist interface is a viable consideration in the network design, just as specialists are trained for word processing centers.

The use of slow-scan video systems (i.e., graphic material depicted on a television screen, but using a telephone bandwidth transmission system) is the subject of Scenario 3. This scenario also shows the utility of a hybrid graphic-audio, real-time system in facilitating informal conferences.

Scenario 4 describes the activities of terminal operators at a dispersed center of the fictitious "Lifetime Insurance Company." They update accounts of clients and use buffer storage in the form of tape cartridges to hold all information generated in the day's work. At the end of the day the stored information is transferred via telephone lines to the central computer facility. The job requires little physical movement; prompts furnished by a minicomputer preclude the necessity for mental involvement. The system is prone to very high error and manpower turnover rates. The task is a typical clerical task. The scenario suggests problem areas that must be kept in mind when the environment for such tasks is designed.

Scenario 5 describes a public telecommunications system. A person at a pay video telephone is pictured as he negotiates with a bank agent for a loan. The agent's terminal access to a computer data base allows him to quickly determine the applicant's credit rating. A printer inside the phone booth generates the necessary documents.

Whether the applicant would have a better (or worse) chance of being granted a loan if he went to the bank in person, and whether the visual channel is needed at all in this type of transaction are central human factor issues of interest in the scenario. A side issue generated by this scenario is whether such a system would significantly alter the loan transaction volume. The legality of documents generated by remote printers is also a matter of concern, since transmission errors may alter the agreed upon negotiations and terms.

Scenario 6 pictures a system of business document generation based on the ultimate organizational diffusion: a secretarial force working from their homes. Any business organization can obtain access to this secretarial force through the contract of their services via a service broker: "Secrepool." Documents to be typed are orally coded on tape by the sender and sent over voice-grade lines to a center that distributes typing jobs to the secretarial force. Upon each job request the center transfers letters to a secretary's tape recorder, again over voice-grade lines. Secretaries use editing typewriters to alphanumerically encode messages on magnetic tape. The recorded messages are sent back to the center via telephone. When a sender wishes to read the typed document, he or she calls the center for a copy and views it through a CRT display. If the document is approved, an electronic signature is entered (by means of a device such as a special graphics pad at the executive's terminal), and the document is electronically sent to central mailing. The information flow process for this scenario is diagrammed in Figure 6.2.

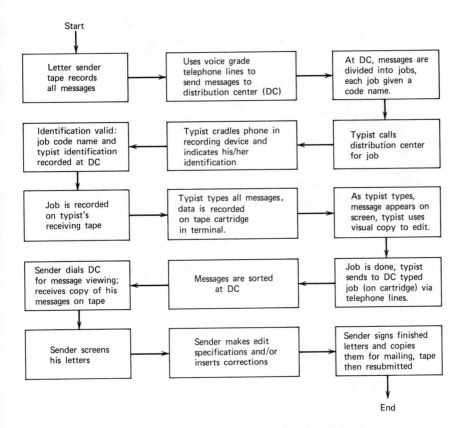

Figure 6.2 Secrepool system: processing new messages.

Again, the possibility of transmission errors brings to light a concern over the legality of the signed documents. The scenario generates another concern common in systems applying telecommunications technology: privacy. Safeguards must be built into such a system to ensure that letters are viewed only by the appropriate system users.

The Secrepool system may require a subdivision whose sole responsibility is revision and/or correction of typed documents. Do people become bored doing fulltime error correction? Is greater work diversity required? A more general question concerns the type of work force a fully dispersed system would attract. Is the typical worker amenable to working at home? Would the worker appreciate the direct and indirect costs savings of this system? Would he or she accept a lower salary in exchange for the ability to work at home?

The following detailed scenarios may elicit other questions and possibilities as the reader considers them. However they may be bypassed if only a general view of the options is desired.

Scenario IA.   J. J. Jones, executive manager of the Benington National Bank, sat down in front of a green CRT. He opened his *User's Guide* and turned to the section "Computer Conferencing System." A table of system commands opened before him.

After glancing at the table, he typed on the keyboard:

JONES 421–92–4213

ENTER CONFERENCE AGENDA

MENU

He followed this with a press of the PROCESS key.

Jones read the screen as it returned the computer's response:

THE DATE IS NOVEMBER 28.

THE TIME IS 9:00.

NO OTHER CONFERENCE MEMBER IS PRESENTLY INTERACTING WITH THE SYSTEM.

IF THIS USER STATUS CHANGES YOU SHALL BE INFORMED.

MENU

DO YOU WISH

1 A SUMMARY OF THE CURRENT STATUS OF CONFERENCE MEMBERS

2 AN UPDATE ON CONFERENCE MESSAGES SINCE YOUR LAST CONFERENCE INTERACTION

3 TO SEND A PRIVATE MESSAGE TO A PARTICULAR MEMBER OR SUBGROUP

4 YOUR PRIVATE MESSAGES

5 A PARTICULAR MESSAGE

PLEASE TYPE THE NUMBER OF YOUR CHOICE*

Jones responded by typing a "1" followed by the process key. The computer returned:

THERE ARE PRESENTLY 124 MESSAGES ON THE CONFERENCE LIST.

THE LAST MESSAGE WAS ENTERED BY SUMNER AT 4:20 PM NOV 27. THE CURRENT STATUS OF THE CONFERENCE IS SUMMARIZED BELOW:

CONFERENCE MEMBER	LAST ON	LAST MESSAGE PROCESSED
GIBBS	9:35 AM NOV 27	107
JONES	9:47 AM NOV 26	100
PETERSON	11:05 AM NOV 27	123
ROSS	10:01 PM NOV 27	125
SUMNER	4:30 PM NOV 27	124*

Jones read the status report and typed "MENU." MENU reappeared on the screen. Jones responded with a "4."

THE FOLLOWING MESSAGES HAVE BEEN SENT TO YOU SINCE NOV 26, 9:47 AM:

SENT 4:15 PM NOV 27

SUMNER—PETERSON SUGGESTS IN MESSAGES 110, 117, 119, 121 THAT THE INKBLOT PEN COMPANY WILL FOLD IN JANUARY. AS YOU WILL SEE, HE USES BANKRUPTCY AS AN ARGUMENT FOR BUYING INTO NEVERDRY PENS. I AM SKEPTICAL. AS I RECALL, YOU KNOW P. C. CURTIS AT INKBLOT. SEE WHAT YOU CAN GET FROM CURTIS BEFORE THE DECEMBER 1 GENERAL MEETING.

NO OTHER MESSAGES.

Jones left the terminal and walked over to the phone, placing his call to P. C. Curtis. Curtis was not in but would return his call shortly. He returned to the terminal and typed "2." Message 101 appeared on the screen along with the name of its author. It was then followed by:

WHEN YOU WISH TO CONTINUE TYPE C

Jones read the message, typed C, and 102 was displayed. He proceeded in this manner until reading message 122. At this point he decided to insert a comment. Glancing at the command table, he typed an IC for insert and continued.

LAST MESSAGE PROCESSED: 122—ROSS WHAT IS YOUR MESSAGE? 126:

Jones' message began

REFERRING TO 122 . . .

Jones read through his message and used an EDIT command to alter part of it before tapping the PROCESS key. Message 123 filled the screen. Jones continued through the conference. Completing 126, he adjoined another comment which became 127. The phone rang. The call from Curtis was through. Jones went to his desk and leaned back in his chair.

"How's business, Pam?" he asked.

Scenario IB. Franklin W. Merriweather seated himself in front of his breakfast of dry toast and black coffee. He unfolded the morning newspaper: "COASTAL BOARD PERMITS EXPANSION OF EDISON FACILITIES AT SAN ONOFRE."

Jill and Jacqueline Merriweather rushed into the kitchen. "Bye, daddy."

They grabbed their lunches and fled through the back door.

The phone rang.

"Hello, darling. Listen, I forgot to tell you that Margaret and Phillip are coming for dinner tonight. Would you take a roast out of the freezer? I won't be home until 4:30 or 5:00. I'm holding a parent conference. If you have time, put the meat in the oven around 4:00."

Frank entered his study. A pile of reports covered his desk.

"I really should file all that stuff," he thought.

As he sifted through the papers, a hand-written note caught his attention: Before Policy Conference on December 12: ANALYZE STATISTICS ON OD ACCOUNTS.

Frank uttered a mild expletive. "I forgot all about this." Turning to the CRT which rested to the right of his desk, he typed:

MERRIWEATHER 653–88–1773 ENTER CONFERENCE POLICY MENU

The computer responded:

THE DATE IS DEC. 12. THE TIME IS 9:04 AM. THE POLICY CONFERENCE WILL BEGIN AT 10:00 AM. THERE IS NO MENU. WOULD YOU LIKE ONE? (YES/NO)*

This time the expletive was slightly stronger.

Frank swung around to his littered desk looking for his *User's Guide.* Before finding it, he remembered the correct call. He turned to the screen. The question still stared at him.

NO

The screen's message faded away. Frank typed:

ENTER CONFERENCE POLICY AGENDA MENU

The computer responded:

THE DATE IS DEC. 12. THE TIME IS 9:13 AM. NO OTHER CONFERENCE MEMBER. . . .

Frank punched the ATTENTION key, abruptly stopping the printout. He then typed "4" and the fading screen renewed itself:

THE FOLLOWING MESSAGES HAVE BEEN SENT TO YOU SINCE DEC 10, 4:32 PM.

SENT 2:00 PM DEC 11

SYMORE MELBOURNE IN MES. 192 SAYS THAT OUR HOME-OWNER'S LOAN PROCEDURE LACKS BRANCH CONSISTENCY. I HAVE NOT BEEN ABLE TO CONVINCE HIM OF THE IMPORTANCE OF REGIONAL INDEPENDENCE. HE IS GOING TO MOVE FOR TIGHTENING.

NO OTHER MESSAGES*

Frank typed "2" and read through new conference messages as they sequenced on the screen. After reading the last message, he again went in search of his *User's Guide*. After shuffling through several drawers and heaps, he sighted it resting on top of the terminal. He grabbed it and fell back into his chair.

"Divisions . . . divisions . . ." he muttered as he thumbed through the guide. A tree indicating the Benington National Bank structure rested below the title DIVISIONS. Frank turned back to the terminal.

ENTER DIVISION CHECK PROCESSING-STATISTICS

The computer responded:

THERE IS NO SUCH LABEL IN OUR LISTING. DID YOU MAKE A TYPING ERROR? (YES/NO)*

NO

The computer answered:

CHECK DIVISION LISTING PAGE 42 of USER'S GUIDE*

Frank chewed his thumbnail and muttered softly. After checking his watch, he picked up the phone and dialed a number. A voice answered, "You have reached network information. Please hold the line. An operator will be with you momentarily."

Music filled the interlude. Jones rocked nervously in his chair. The voice broke the melody.

"Please hold the line. An operator will be with you momentarily."

Frank slammed the phone back in its cradle, terminating a saccharine version of "Up, Up and Away." He spun around and stared at the terminal.

CHECK DIVISION LISTING PAGE 42 of USER'S GUIDE*

Franklin W. Merriweather started on the other thumbnail as he checked the manual again. "Maybe I made a typing error," he mumbled. He retyped:

ENTER DIVISION CHECK PROCESSING-STATISTICS

and the computer responded promptly:

THERE IS NO SUCH LABEL IN OUR LISTING. DID YOU MAKE A TYPING ERROR? (YES/NO)*

NO DAMNIT

Frank glared at the screen as it printed:

NO DAMNIT NOT A VALID COMMAND. PLEASE ANSWER YES OR NO.

Frank Merriweather was now audibly abusive. He grabbed the telephone again and dialed.

"You have reached network information. Please hold the line. An operator will be with you momentarily."

Scenario 2. "Myra, could you send this memo out to all the other divisions, please?"

"Yes, Mr. Hart."

As she typed the memo on her terminal, the words appeared on the viewing screen before her.

MEMO FROM COLLECTIONS DIVISION OF THE J.T.C. INSURANCE COMPANY

TO ALL DIVISIONS

CONCERNING NEW POLICY ON LATE PAYMENTS

DUE TO THE INCREASING NUMBER OF OUR CUSTOMERS WHO ARE MAKING PAYMENTS THREE TO FOUR DAYS PAST THE DEADLINE, WE ARE EXTENDING . . .

After proofreading her copy, she typed in the send commands and waited for the signal telling her that it had been received by all the divisions. Then she punched the store instruction and the memo was dated and recorded in the central data files.

As the images faded away, a new message appeared:

REQUEST FROM ACCOUNTING DEPARTMENT FOR FILE OF EXPENSES INCURRED PREVIOUS MONTH.

Myra stood up and walked over to the cabinet which stored all the magnetic tapes. As she was looking for the correct tape, Bob, who handled overdue payments, came up to her.

"Hi, Myra, how are you doing?"

"Oh, all right, I guess, except for my asthma and the poison ivy. I went to see the doctor Tuesday and he said that . . ."

"Uh, Myra, when you have a free minute, could you send out for the file on John Butler, account number G97423–B?"

"Sure, I'll have it for you in a few minutes."

"Thanks, I'll be back to pick it up."

Myra found the right tape and mounted it on a tape drive. Then she seated herself back at the terminal.

ATTENTION ACCOUNTING DEPARTMENT

SIGNAL WHEN READY TO RECEIVE BULK INFORMATION
TRANSFER

READY

Within seconds, the transfer was completed.

By the time the request for information had been filled, Bob was
back to pick up the newly printed output. Myra was now faced with
the choice of either updating the current list of overdue payments or
cross-checking today's collections with the bank to find the bad
checks. Since it was nearly lunchtime, she decided upon the former.

UPDATE ON FILE OF OVERDUE PAYMENTS

TO CENTRAL DATA FILES

FOLLOWING—LIST OF PAYMENTS RECEIVED TO DATE
FILE 382–C

SEND AND RESPOND

As she finished typing one of the tape drives started up and soon
after the card puncher started producing reminders to be mailed.

"Hey, Myra, ready for lunch?"

"Sure Sophie, soon as I collect these cards. Italian or the new taco
place?"

Myra finished collecting the cards, typed a message, and left.

COLLECTIONS DIVISION INACCESSIBLE.

OUT TO LUNCH.

Scenario 3.   As he turned over, rays of sunlight broke his sleep. He
jabbed a button on the clock radio.

". . . closing the trade, Campanis predicted that the summer would
be a hot one indeed. This is Herb Martin from the world of sports . . .
and this is radio K-WOW. It's 2:35 and a big, bright, beautiful Tuesday
afternoon. . . ."

He was out of coffee filters and hunted through the garbage can for
a used one. Finding one in an empty milk carton, he fished it out, carefully rinsed it, and folded it into the coffee pot. The water wasn't
ready, so he walked over to the phone and dialed the library.

"Hello . . . this morning I dialed for microfilm reference 42328, and
it didn't come through . . . when did I call? About 3 AM . . . but my
indicator light didn't go on. . . . I'll have it checked then. When will
the system be up again? . . . OK, I'll dial for it."

As he drank his coffee, he read through the papers covering the
table. Setting down the last page he smiled. "Coates will like this."

John Coates leaned back in his swivel chair. As he stretched his arms behind his head, he thought about taking a short nap. He had been working since 9 AM and was beginning to tire. He opened the door of his study. Through the living room window he could see Mary, his wife, backing the car out of the driveway. The phone in his study rang.

"Hello."

"Hello, Dr. Coates. This is Sam. I did some work this morning that I'd like you to see."

"OK, Sam." Coates flipped on the screen above the phone carriage.

"This follows directly from our latest results on p-adic L functions. I think Tate may have conjectured it in a lecture series, but the library was down this morning so I couldn't check."

As Sam·wrote the theorem and its proof on a white surface it was beamed back to Coates. Sam's explanation was broken several times as Coates modified or questioned the steps.

"That's good, Sam. It should be in your dissertation, so you had better check Tates' work. . . . You know, this suggests that functions satisfying this property might be constructed in the following way. . . ."

As Sam turned on his screen, Coates' message began to sprawl across it. Sam began to take down some notes.

"OK, I'll try it. I'll call you back if it works. By the way, I dialed in for your seminar lecture yesterday. It was quite good. . . ."

They went on to discuss the seminar, exchanging more ideas over the video channel. Breaking a concluding pause, Sam said, "I think I'll go have some breakfast."

I'm going to be occupied this evening," Coates said. "If anything develops, call me tomorrow."

Coates hung up the phone, pressing the NOT AVAILABLE button on its carriage. "Guess I'll take that nap," he thought.

Scenario 4.   Paula stepped into the last available space of the elevator.

"42 please," she said to the elevator attendant.

As she stepped out of the elevator she heard someone call her name. It was Sharon.

"Hi, Sharon. Did you have a good time last night?"

"Oh, it was okay, I guess."

Sharon and Paula walked down the red-carpeted corridor. Sharon stopped in front of a door addressed: Benington First National Bank—Check Processing Division. She turned to Paula before entering.

"Lunch?"

"Sure."

Paula continued down the corridor to the last office of the wing: Lifetime Insurance—Policy Updating Division. Opening the door, she was met by the commotion of morning ritual. She walked over to a crowded mailbox area. In the cubbyhole addressed to her, she found a brown paper packet.

"Hi, Paula."

"Hi, Kathy."

Kathy found her packet and they both walked down an aisle bordered by 30 CRT terminal stations. They reached their neighboring stations and were quickly seated. Paula opened her packet, pulling out a cartridge of microfiche. She put the cartridge into a reader which rested to the right of her terminal keyboard. A series of images of checks filled the screen as she turned on the reader. Beneath the signature of each check was a series of numbers indicating the signee's account number. Paula turned on the terminal and typed:

JENKINS 1672–45–2241 RECORD UPDATING—POLICY FORM 2018

The computer responded:

ENTER ACCOUNT NUMBER/INFORMATION CODE*

After looking at the first check, Paula typed:

41721/24

The computer responded:

ENTER AMOUNT*

Paula typed:

$78.97

and the cycle began again with

ENTER ACCOUNT NUMBER/

Before entering the next number, Paula turned to Kathy and said, "Muriel and Will are seeing each other again."

"No," said Kathy. "Really? What's Sally going to do about it?"

When Paula finished the next update, she turned to Kathy. "I don't know," she said. "I don't think she'll give Will a divorce."

Kathy finished the first page of microfiche and pushed the PAGE button of her reader. A new series of checks filled the screen. "She should. Honestly, she's the one who broke up Muriel and Will in the first place. It was a good marriage before *she* came along."

"Yeah, but Will is very attached to the baby and if he goes back to Muriel, Sally won't let him have Johnny."

Kathy was about to reply but Paula stopped her. "Wait a minute."

Paula looked at the number at the corner of the screen and the number indexing the check she was presently processing. They coincided.

"OK, go on. I thought I had skipped one."

Kathy punched PAGE again and said: "Well, you know, Will wouldn't be so attached to that baby if he knew it wasn't his."

"What!" said Paula.

"Sure," replied Kathy. "Didn't you know that? That baby is Hank's."

"Hank? Will's brother!!?"

"Sure," said Kathy.

"But Hank's such a creep! Did you . . ."

"Wait," said Kathy. "I just entered the right amount on the wrong account." She pressed the CHECK button on her terminal and the entire series of accounts she had processed from the microfiche page appeared on the screen, each number followed by the money entry she had typed. She checked the microfiche accounts with those on the CRT and said,

"No, it's right. What were you going to say?"

"Well," said Paula. "I was just going to tell you that that creep joined Hades' Angels."

Scenario 5.   Mr. Hart had been at this video phone often to obtain his bank statements, but this time it was different. He was worried. He wanted a loan.

He put in his quarter and dialed the number of his bank. A young woman's face appeared.

"United American Bank. Good morning. May I help you?"

"My name is Jonathan Hart and I would like to talk to someone about a loan."

"One moment, please, Mr. Hart, and I will connect you with our Loan Department."

A picture of the United American Bank appeared on the screen as Mr. Hart was put on hold. In about 30 seconds, a new face materialized.

"Russ Johnson is my name, Mr. Hart. Now what seems to be the problem today?"

As Johnson listened, he could see Hart on the upper part of his screen, while on the lower half, data describing Hart's account with the bank began flashing onto the screen.

HART, JONATHAN T.

ACCOUNT NUMBER 025–69801–05

CURRENT SAVINGS BALANCE	$697.83
CURRENT CHECKING BALANCE	$187.51
AVERAGE MONTHLY BALANCE	$150.28
NUMBER OF OVERDRAWN CHECKS	0

After Hart had finished, Johnson started in with the usual questions:

"Have you ever had a loan granted before?"

"Sure. I had a federally insured loan of $500 while attending college. I paid that back as soon as I started working."

This was confirmed on his viewing screen. Johnson now began typing in the details about Hart: family status, job, income, former employers, and so on. As this was being completed, the results of the computerized credit check began coming in.

HART, JONATHAN T.   692–58–6211   NO BAD CHECKS

MAJOR CREDIT CARDS

    BANKAMERICARD $300/MO LIMIT   GOOD RECORD

    MAY CO   GOOD RECORD

    SHELL OIL CO   GOOD RECORD

"Well, Mr. Hart, you have never had a major loan before, but you seem to be a good risk. I think we can grant this loan request. Now, let me calculate the different monthly rates for you."

As the figures appeared on his screen, Johnson read them off to Hart.

LOAN OF $10,000.00

    $1,000/MONTH FOR 11 MONTHS

    500/MONTH FOR 23 MONTHS

    250/MONTH FOR 47 MONTHS

    125/MONTH FOR 95 MONTHS

    75/MONTH FOR 160 MONTHS

They discussed which payment schedule would be best for him and decided upon the optimum monthly payment. When the details had been clarified, copies of the agreement were printed up at the video phone automatically. Hart would sign one and mail it back to the bank and the money would then be deposited into his account.

"Well, Mr. Hart. Thank you for doing business with U.A.B."

Scenario 6. "Hello . . . Secrepool Distribution Center . . ."

"Hello, this is Jim Nehring at You Bet Your Life Insurance. We just joined the Secrepool system and I'm a little confused about the telephone numbers you sent us."

"Mr. Nehring, each telephone number is associated with a different mailing priority. Your monthly bill is based on the distribution of use of the different numbers. For example, if you want messages processed and mailed immediately, it will cost you more than if there is no rush on the materials."

". . . and furthermore, You Bet Your Life Insurance cannot . . . cannot . . ." Nehring leaned back in his chair. Pressing the WAIT button on his recorder, he stopped the tape that was collecting his message. He left the room and returned with a cup of coffee. He snapped the recorder on again and continued. Finishing the letter, he dialed one of Secrepool's numbers. After putting the phone head in its place on the recorder and depressing several buttons of the phone carriage to indicate his identification, the letter was transferred to the Secrepool Bank.

Johnny entered the kitchen. "I don't feel so great," he said.

His mother leaned over him and felt his warm forehead. "Hmmmm. Better not go to school today."

She tucked him into his bed and went back to the kitchen. After putting some coffee water on, she went to the study and dialed a number on the telephone. She waited for the signal and placed the handset on a recording device. The device automatically activated. She returned to the kitchen and poured the coffee. By the time she returned to the study the recorder had automatically rewound the tape and turned itself off.

Putting on the headset, she began typing the first letter. As she typed, the message appeared on a screen resting above the keyboard. The letter done, she proofread it and then pressed the FILE key of her keyboard. The letter disappeared, its contents recorded on the terminal's tape cartridge.

After typing the last letter on the tape, she took the cartridge out of the terminal. Placing it in the recorder, she dialed Secrepool's distribution center and transferred her finished work. As her son wailed for orange juice and affection, she left the room.

It was 8 AM and Nehring reached the office early. He went to his phone and dialed a Secrepool number. After identifying himself he turned on his recorder and placed the phone head in place. Copies of his typed letters were taped. He placed the cartridge in his terminal, turned it on, and a letter filled the screen. He read it through and picked up an electronic pencil. He inserted his signature and pressed the MAIL key. A new letter filled the screen.

The information flow pattern for this scenario is charted in Figure 6.2.

REFERENCES

1. Communications Studies Group, Joint Unit for Planning Research. *Electronic Person-to-Person Communications: An Interim Report of a Pilot Study.* London: Communications Studies Group, University College, 1970.

2. Communications Studies Group, Joint Unit for Planning Research. *Miscellaneous Papers Submitted to the Steering Committee.* London: Communications Study Group, University College, 1971.

3. A. E. Stahmer and M. D. Havron. *Planning Research in Teleconferencing Systems.* A report prepared for the Social Policy and Programs Branch, The Department of Communications, Ottawa, Canada. McLean: Human Sciences Research, Inc., September, 1973.

Chapter 7

Transportation and Energy Costs

The key factor for both the decentralization decision by an organization and the formulation of public policy is the cost advantage (or disadvantage) of telecommuting over commuting using transportation. Consequently the determination of employee commuting distances was integral to the study. With these data the research team (a) had a basis for selection of the dispersed center locations; (b) calculated the costs of commuting for the insurance company employees; (c) estimated the energy costs associated with commuting; and (d) defined the savings in mileage and energy that were possible with a dispersed telecommunications network. This chapter is concerned with the costs—both in dollars and energy—of commuting. All calculations were based on costs of energy and the costs of owning and operating an automobile in January, 1974. The costs presented here are not to be taken as established, scientifically accurate factors but rather as estimators of the relative current prices of these two activities. The telecommuting dollar costs were estimated in Chapter 5.

BASELINE DATA

To calculate the costs of commuting for the insurance company employees, residence data (by ZIP code) were obtained from the insurance company for 2048 employees (81% of the total number). These data were broken down by employee grade level. Since ZIP codes in the Los Angeles area cover relatively small geographic areas, the centroid of each ZIP code area served as a convenient accumulation point for calculations. The insurance company employees were distributed throughout 212 different ZIP code areas (distribution is shown in Figure 4.5).

The travel distance to the central downtown site was computed for each ZIP code area by assuming that employees would use the Los Angeles freeway system (Figure 7.1) if a freeway were available between the ZIP code area and the headquarters. The results of this analysis, by employee grade level, are shown in Table 7.1. The one-way weighted average commuting distance the medians, and modes are given for each category of employee. The average one-way distance for all employees was 10.7 miles, a figure only slightly higher (15%) than the national average one-way commute of 9.4 miles in major metropolitan areas [7.1].

DOLLAR COSTS FOR COMMUTING

In calculating the costs associated with commuting, it was assumed that the insurance company employees' purchasing habits conform

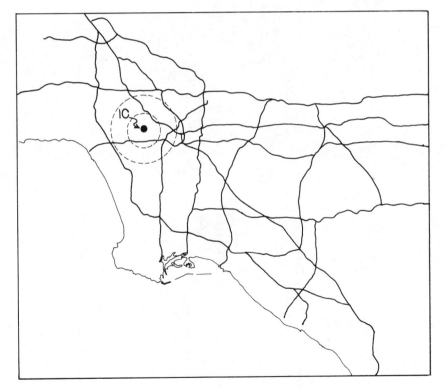

Figure 7.1   Los Angeles freeway system.

Table 7.1. Insurance Company Locational Analysis

Class	Job Level Categories	Percent of Employees	One-Way Weighted Average Distance in Miles	Median	Mode	Standard Deviation
Executives	20–84	6	16.6	17	22	18.9
Middle Management	7–12	27	13.3	13	18	16.3
Clerical Workers	1–6	67	9.3	8	3	11.8
All Employees		100	10.7	9	3	13.5

reasonably closely to those of the national average [7.2]. Information on the costs of automobile ownership and operation was compiled from several sources [7.3–7.5] and adjusted for inflation and the USC study conditions.

Table 7.2 shows the results of the cost estimates for the operation of a private automobile, using the average round trip distance (21.4 miles) calculated for the employees. Two cases are illustrated: the first in which the commuter uses the car solely for commuting and the second in which commuting use, assuming a single-car household, covers only 50% of the automobile's total use. In the second case only those costs specifically attributable to commuting were used in the estimate. Calculations were done for both compact and subcompact cars.

Table 7.2. Direct Operating Costs of Private Auto Commuting

	Average Annual Cost ($)			
	Commuter Use Only		50% Commuter Use[a]	
Cost Element	Standard	Subcompact	Standard	Subcompact
Depreciation	643	302	not applicable	
Financing	166	99	not applicable	
Maintenance	315	260	158	130
Gasoline,Oil[b]	260	145	252	138
Insurance	198	183	15 (est.)	14
Parking[c]	450	450	450	450
Taxes	75	45	not applicable	
Total costs	2173	1538	875	732
Total cost per commuter[d]	1671	1183	673	563
Composite cost per commuter[e]	1573		651	

[a] All figures shown are costs attributable solely to commuting. Costs that the owner would have to bear even if the use for commuting were discontinued (and ownership were continued) are not included. Except for gasoline and oil, all costs are based on 1972 prices.

[b] Gasoline prices of $0.53 per gallon and fuel consumptions of 11 and 22 miles per gallon are assumed for the standard and subcompact cars, respectively.

[c] Parking costs are not necessarily paid directly by the employee, as are other costs. The figure used is the equivalent cost of off-street parking in typical large metropolitan areas.

[d] At 1.3 persons per automobile.

[e] This assumes 80% standard, 20% subcompact mix.

In the composite cost per commuter a mix of 80% standard and 20% subcompacts was assumed. The total and composite costs are both based on a presumed car occupancy of 1.3 persons per vehicle, the national average for all purposes [7.6], although the average occupancy rate per commuter vehicle for Los Angeles is even lower at 1.1 persons per vehicle. Presumably, the national average commuter auto occupancy is also about 1.1 persons per vehicle, at least in major, metropolitan areas. However, the higher figure was used here to ensure conservatism [7.7]. Finally, it should be noted that parking costs are often included as a direct cost borne by the employee, although in the case of the insurance company under study the company bears this cost. However, at least 54% of the drivers who commute to work in the Los Angeles central business district pay for their parking on an average weekday [7.8] and therefore bear the cost directly.

The total costs of commuting were calculated for the 2517 insurance company employees based on the estimated costs of owning and operating a car to commute the 21.4 miles round trip to the insurance company. It was assumed that the insurance company employees had approximately the same distribution of single and multiple car households and households without automobile ownership as did the general population of the urban United States at the time of the 1970 census [7.9].

This ownership distribution was 54.1% (single car ownership), 37.7% (multiple car ownership), and 17.2% (no automobile ownership). Using this distribution, the total annual commuting costs for 2048 employees for whom we had residence data amounted to $1,816,000. If the same distribution of ownership and use is assumed for the 469 employees for whom we did not have residence data, the total annual commuting costs for the insurance company employees were $2,232,000 in 1974. The average cost of commuting for the 82.8% of the employees presumed to drive their automobiles to work equals $1071 per employee. This can be expressed as approximately 22 cents per mile, including parking costs, for these employees to commute. When the parking costs are excluded for the insurance company employees, the transportation cost borne by the employee drops to 15 cents per mile, and the annual cost borne by the employee is $714.

These calculations do not include the commuting cost for the 17.2% of the insurance company employee population that does not own an automobile. It may be assumed that these employees either walk or use forms of transportation (bus, taxi, bicycle) for which no average cost can be determined without exhaustive research.

The preceding factors represent, aside from the number of employees used as a basis for calculation, a hypothetical model. In actuality the assumption of 1.3 passengers per vehicle is not accurate for the insurance company employees. These employees, like other Los Angelenos, tend to drive alone, averaging 1.08 or fewer passengers per vehicle, a difference of about 20%. Elimination of 0.2 passengers per vehicle in the cost-of-operation calculations roughly compensates for the 17.2% of the employees who were assumed, in the previous calculations, to have used alternate means to arrive at work. If the figures are used of 2517 employees who commute an average of 10.7 miles one way daily for a 230-day working year, the number of miles traveled each year by the insurance company employees totals approximately 12,400,000. On the basis of 1.1 passengers per vehicle and an average cost of 22 cents per passenger mile, the costs of commuting for the employees would be approximately $2,730,000 annually. Again, since the employees are not charged for parking, their annual portion of the total transportation cost is $1,850,000.

ENERGY COSTS

One interesting aspect of the potential substitution of telecommunications technology for transportation is the impact on national energy use. In view of the recent emphasis on energy issues at the national level, especially those related to transportation, it is important that this factor in the tradeoff be seriously considered. Although the question of energy use has recently come into widespread national prominence, the historical abundance of various forms of energy has resulted in a fairly general ignorance of the details of energy consumption of various human activities. This historically perceived abundance of energy has also resulted in the underpricing of most energy supplies for some time.

Consequently the researcher is faced with two problems in developing accurate comparisons of the relative energy uses of transportation and telecommunications. First, very little information is available about the detailed energy costs of production and maintenance, as opposed to the operation, of the equipment and systems constituting the subject alternatives. Second, the cost of energy is rising rapidly in some sectors of the economy, less rapidly in others, so that the only definite statement we can make at this time is that these costs are in upward flux.

Hence the following estimates of relative energy consumption and cost of transportation and telecommunications are based on the best data available in 1975. For the most part the estimates are limited to the relative operating energy consumption of transportation and tele-commuting in the urban environment. Since energy cost and consumption figures vary considerably in different publications, the estimates are intended to indicate the relative differences in costs and should not be considered as highly precise evaluations.

National Transportation Energy Costs

Estimates for total transportation operating energy use range from 23.8% to 25.2% of gross national energy use [7.10, 7.11]. This proportion of gross national energy use is expected to remain relatively constant for the next few years. We have assumed a value of 25% for our calculations. This value is translated into quadrillion British thermal units (Quad) as 17 Quad in 1971 and 19 Quad in 1975, as the gross national energy consumption for transportation.

Automobile transportation constitutes approximately 50% of all transportation usage according to Hirst [7.12]. Urban automobile usage accounted for 34.2% of all transportation energy use in 1970 [7.13]. Linear extrapolation of Hirst's data indicates an urban automobile usage of 36.7% in 1975. The above estimate for total transportation use amounts to 9.2% of total energy consumption in the United States for 1975.

Data developed from various sources indicate that commuting accounts for approximately 42% of all urban automobile transportation mileage or 3.9% of total energy consumption for the United States [7.14]. Conversely, commuting can be said to account for 25.4% of U.S. transportation energy consumption. If these percentages of use devoted to commuting were to remain constant, we could say that commuting accounted for the expenditure of 2.6 Quad in 1971 and, if unaltered in character, will account for 5 Quad in the year 2000. Consequently each percent reduction in urban commuting in the 1975 to 1980 era would result in a total U.S. energy conservation increase of more than 30 trillion Btu annually. In electrical terms a 1% reduction in urban commuting would result in a reduction in total U.S. energy consumption of approximately 8.6 billion kilowatt-hours annually.

Case Study Transportation Energy

The insurance company employees' average daily commute of 21.4 miles round trip was used as the basis for estimating the energy consumption of an individual commuter. Although slightly higher than the national average round trip commute of 18.8 miles, the insurance company average was considered to be representative of the daily commute for white-collar workers in a major metropolitan area.

To develop a basis for comparsion we calculated the operating energy costs for the automobiles used by the insurance company employees. These energy costs, as estimated by Hirst in 1973 (expressed in Btu per passenger mile) [7.15], were converted to kilowatt-hours. There are 3413 Btu per kilowatt-hour. Using the Los Angeles Regional Transportation Study estimate of 1.1 passengers per commuter vehicle mile and 230 working days a year for 2517 employees, we calculated the total annual energy use by the employees for commuting to be approximately 37.4 million kilowatt-hours.

If we further assume, on the basis of the Los Angeles experience, that the nationwide average loading of a private automobile used for urban commuting is also 1.1 passengers, we find, at 11,340 Btu per vehicle mile [7.16], that the average urban commuter consumes 64.6 kilowatt-hours per day. Using Hirst's data for energy consumption for mass transit systems (mostly buses), we find equivalent energy consumptions of 24.1 kilowatt-hours per day for each commuter for normally loaded mass transit (a load factor of 20%) [7.17]. A fully loaded mass transit system, that is, one in which all available spaces were always occupied by commuters, would use 4.8 kilowatt-hours per day for each commuter. In practice no such highly conservative system exists.

Telecommuting Energy

We arrive at comparable costs for telecommuting by noting that a typical computer terminal continuously uses 100 to 125 watts, or less, when it is in operation. A 4-kilohertz bandwidth phone line uses less than 1 watt once the connection is established in a typical urban area (there is an initial 10 to 15 watt power consumption in a switched network used for the ringing circuits). The marginal costs of computer and peripheral equipment operation per terminal are estimated at approrimately 10 watts. If we postulate a terminal use and/or "connect" (to the computer) time of 5 hours per day, a considerably higher figure than present experience with the insurance company, we arrive at a total energy consumption of 0.68 kilowatt-hours per day for each telecommuter. However, this figure is the delivered electrical energy to the telecommuter. Therefore we must put in an additional conversion factor to refer the energy cost back to input fossil fuel energy required at the central, conventional electrical power plant that provides the primary energy for telecommuting. Thus we end up with a value of 2.2 kilowatt-hours per day for each telecommuter as the gross basic energy requirement. This estimate is quite conservative since our survey of insurance company employees indicates that each employee could take care of data transmission needs with about 10 minutes of terminal time. We inflated this time to include new uses of the terminal, for example, development of "paperless" office systems, electronic mail, remote job training, and remote supervision.

Relative Energy Consumption

From these estimates we find that the relative energy consumption advantage of telecommuting over commuting (i.e., the ratio of commuting energy consumption to telecommuting consumption) is at least 29:1 when the private automobile is used, 11:1 when normally loaded mass transit is used, and 2:1 for 100% utilized mass transit systems (Figure 7.2). However, since most urban passenger traffic (approximately 97%) now uses the automobile, we find that the net savings in energy consumption produced by telecommuting is 96% of the fraction of commuting replaced. Consequently, in the United States the

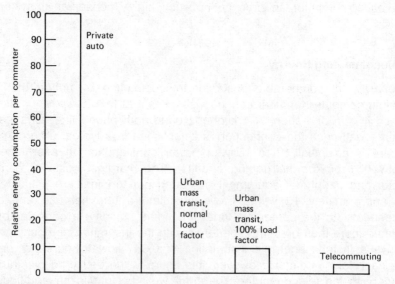

Figure 7.2 Relative energy consumption of intraurban commuting. Transportation energy costs are taken from E. Hirst, *Energy Intensiveness of Passenger and Freight Transportation Modes* and uses 1950–1970 model mixes. Telecommuting includes electrical power plant losses.

replacement of urban commuting by telecommuting (at least telecommuting carried out at telephone bandwidths) would result in a net energy consumption reduction of 8.2 billion kilowatt-hours annually for each percent of the urban commuting work force engaging in the substitution.

As another example of the energy savings available from telecommunications substitutions for transportation, we can look at a case of the use of USC's Interactive Instructional Television (IITV) System (described in Chapter 9). During a 1975 course entitled "Energy Alternatives" 147 students "attended" the televised lectures at sites located as far as 25 miles from the main campus. If these students had attended the course on campus, instead of using the remote sites, and had adhered to the usual car pooling ratio of 1.1 passengers per auto, they would have expended 15,000 kilowatt-hours of energy per lecture. The marginal costs of operating the IITV, referred to basic fuel energy at the electric power plant, were 9 kilowatt-hours per lecture, giving an energy consumption ratio between the two alternatives of 1700:1.

Since most transportation energy related to commuting is derived from the use of petroleum, we can translate these results to annual savings in terms of barrels of gasoline. At 125,000 Btu per gallon of gasoline and 42 gallons per barrel, we have an energy value of 1539 kilowatt-hours per barrel of gasoline [7.18]. Consequently, a 1% replacement of urban commuting by telecommuting in the United States would result in a net reduction in gasoline consumption of 5.36 million barrels annually. To gain some perspective on the meaning of this, we note that total gasoline imports of the United States in August, 1975, were 277,000 barrels per day, with an estimated 63,000,000 barrels over the entire year. In 1974 U.S. gasoline imports averaged 204,000 barrels per day, or 74,400,000 barrels per year [7.19, 7.20]. Thus replacement of 11.8% in 1975, or 14.0% of urban commuting by telecommuting in 1974 would have eliminated the U.S. requirement for imported gasoline; assuming, of course, that all such imports would ordinarily have been used for automobile consumption rather than other purposes. However, telecommuting would not have eliminated the requirements for importation of crude oil and other refined petroleum products.

Relative Energy Prices

Although the fairly high energy consumption advantage of telecommuting over commuting may exert a moral persuasion for potential users of telecommuting, it is important to recognize that unless external inducements such as rationing are imposed cost savings in dollar terms are likely to be even more persuasive to the individual commuter.

Using Hirst's more conservative values for the energy content of gasoline (136,000 Btu per gallon as opposed to the federal figures of 125,000 Btu per gallon [7.18, 7.21]), we find that the cost per kilowatt-hour for gasoline is $0.0251 \times$ the price per gallon. That is, for gasoline at 55 cents per gallon, the energy price is 1.38 cents per kilowatt-hour. This current price for gasoline energy can be compared with a national average of 1.69 cents per kilowatt-hour for delivered electrical energy in 1971, the latest year for which we have national data [7.22]. The late 1975 price from the Los Angeles Department of Water and Power, for home use, was 3.18 cents per kilowatt-hour. The average price of gasoline to the consumer hovered around 60 cents per gallon, or 1.75 cents per kilowatt-hour in the same period.

Since the ratio between energy consumption for commuting and delivered electrical energy for telecommuting is at least 95:1, we find that the differing prices of the two forms of energy result in an energy price ratio ranging from a national value of 82:1, to 52:1 for Los Angeles in late 1975. Thus, even though the price paid by the consumer per kilowatt-hour is higher for electrical energy than for energy provided by gasoline, the energy price ratio between commuting and telecommuting is higher than the energy consumption ratio. This is because our energy consumption figures are based on total fuel energy used in the process, while the price figures are based on the delivered energy.

As gasoline prices increase, the price advantage of telecommuting can be expected to continue to increase, since the fuel costs constitute almost the entirety of the commuting energy cost while the fuel cost is only a fraction of the telecommuting energy cost (power plant operation, capital equipment amortization, etc., constitute a larger proportion of the costs).

It should be noted, however, that because energy prices constitute a fairly small proportion of the total direct costs of commuting, and an even smaller fraction of telecommuting costs to the individual business firm, they cannot be expected to exert a profound economic influence on the decision by a firm to disperse through the use of telecommunications. Rationing or other restriction of the gasoline supply, for example, is much more likely to sway this decision. Executives from several companies interviewed during the course of our research divulged preliminary plans to develop rudimentary telecommuting systems, at least for some of their fellow executives. These plans were made primarily because of the threat of unavailability of gasoline supplies for individuals located at long distances from the central office, not because of the cost of these supplies to either the firms or the individuals. However, the energy cost ratios may provide a persuasive argument for developing a new view of government policies in fuel allocation, distribution and price control.

Specific Energy Cost Savings

The savings in energy and transportation costs can be dramatically illustrated by considering the decrease in round trip mileage for the employees of the insurance company produced by the presence of up to 35 new work centers throughout the city. As shown in Figure 7.3, the average one way mileage per employee would decrease from 10.7 miles to 3.1 miles, with comparable reductions in energy and transportation costs. The energy and cost savings are shown in Figure 7.4.

Figure 7.3 also illustrates that after addition of the eighteenth cen-

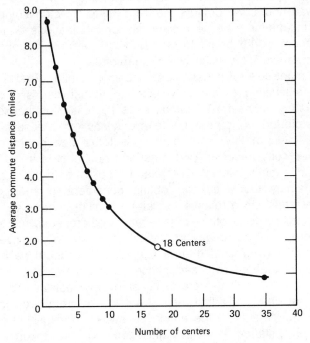

Figure 7.3 Average commute distance vs. number of centers.

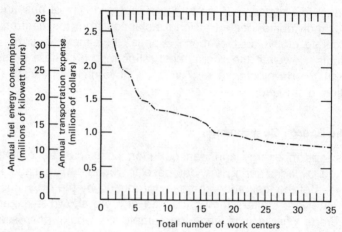

Figure 7.4 Estimated annual commuting costs for insurance company.

ter the decrease in commuter mileage is very gradual. With 18 centers, the average one way distance per employee would be 3.9 miles, with an approximate annual savings in transportation energy of 23.8 million kilowatt-hours. In addition, the fixed costs of establishing 35 centers and maintaining the necessary telecommunications equipment at each of them would begin to outweigh the savings in transportation and energy costs, as is discussed in Chapter 8.

At this point several observations should be made. First, Figure 7.4 indicates a leveling of the curve starting at between six and seven centers, rather than at 18 centers, as is the case for the commuting distances plotted in Figure 7.3. The energy savings, measured in basic fuel cost, even at the seven-center level are enough to equal the annual electricity needs of 360 American households in 1975 [7.23]. One would expect this kind of relationship to hold for many companies; namely that they can obtain considerable energy savings through establishing a relatively small number of centers.

Second, aside from other considerations, there does not appear to be an energy cost advantage to having more than four or five employees use a single terminal (Figure 7.5). Third, it should be noted that the above calculations represent conservative estimates of the savings.

Fourth, it is difficult to determine, or even guess at, the operative reactions of the individual employee to the reduced commuting mileage requirements. If the employee owns more than one car, the reduction in distance to work might encourage him to divest himself

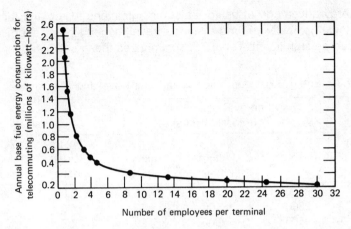

Figure 7.5   Insurance company telecommuting energy costs. This assumes an employee population of 2517; terminal, peripherals, communications line consumption: 160 Watts; 8 hour use time per day per terminal; basic fuel energy equals 3.3 × delivered electrical energy; 230 day work year, terminals off during nonworking hours.

of one of those cars. For employees who own only one car, considerable savings could be realized in terms of automobile operation costs. If both sets of car owners converted to bicycling or walking the shortened distance to work, the savings would be even greater, not to mention secondary benefits, such as the increase in physical health of the employees.

Other Transportation Energy Tradeoffs

Dickson and Bowers [7.24] have performed some rough calculations on energy conservation aspects of the use of the video telephone as a substitute for jet transportation over long distances. They indicate that the ratio of energy use varies between 2.7:1 and 8:1, depending on the contact time between individual participants in a face-to-face (with one taking a jet) or video telephone-to-video telephone discussions. Using the same path (New York to Los Angeles), but substituting computer terminals and telephone bandwidth transmission lines for the video telephone, we calculate that the energy use ratio between jet transportation and long distance telecommuting is 330 (as opposed to 2.7) for 24 hours of contact time. If the contact time is reduced to 8 hours, the jet travel/telecommuting energy use ratio increases to 990 (as opposed to a ratio of 8.0 for the jet travel/video telephone). Thus the energy advantage of using telecommunications to replace face-to-face meetings involving long distance travel, especially for short meetings, can be significant. Table 7.3 summarizes these calculations.

Table 7.3. Energy Costs for Long Distance Jet Travel and Telecommuting

Contact Time (Hours)	Energy Requirements (Kilowatt Hours)			Ratios	
	Boeing[a] 747	Picture-phone[a]	Telecom-muting	747 to Picture-phone	747 to Telecom-muting
8	9500	1200	9.6	8.0	990
16	9500	2400	19	4.0	500
24	9500	3600	29	2.7	330

[a] Energy Requirements and Ratios for Boeing 747 and Picturephone (Registered Service Mark of the American Telephone and Telegraph Company) are taken from Dickson and Bowers, Reference 7.24. Required Picturephone data rate is 1.5 Mbps while telecommuting data rate is 4.8 kbps (simultaneous two-way).

REFERENCES

1   Automobile Manufacturers Association, Inc. *1971 Automobile Facts and Figures*. Detroit: Automobile Manufacturers Association, Inc., 1971, p. 52.

2. L. L. Liston and C. L. Gauthier. *Costs of Operating an Automobile*. Washington, D.C.: U.S. Department of Transportation, Federal Highway Administration, Office of Highway Planning, Highway Statistics Division, April, 1972, pp. 3–5.

3. *Ibid.*

4. U.S. Bureau of the Census. *Statistical Abstract of the United States*. Washington, D.C.: Government Printing Office, 1972, p. 548.

5. Automobile Manufacturers Association, Inc., *op. cit.,* pp. 46–48.

6. *Ibid.*, p. 52.

7. Los Angeles Regional Transportation Study. *Base Year Report: 1971 Origin-Destination Survey*. Los Angeles: Los Angeles Regional Transportation Study, December, 1971, p. 70.

8. *Ibid.*, p. 72.

9. Automobile Manufactures Association, Inc., *op. cit.*, p. 46.

10. Eric Hirst. *Energy Intensiveness of Passenger and Freight Transport Modes, 1950–1970*. Oak Ridge: Oak Ridge National Laboratory, April 1973. Report #ORNL–NSF–EP–44, p. 4.

11. Stanford Research Institute. *Patterns of Energy Consumption in the United States*. Washington, D.C.: Government Printing Office, 1972.

12. Hirst, *op. cit.*, p. 4.

13. *Ibid.*, p. 24.

14. Automobile Manufacturers Association, Inc., *op. cit.*, p. 52.

15. Hirst, *op. cit.,* p. 27.

16. Eric Hirst. *Direct and Indirect Energy Requirements for Automobiles.* Oak Ridge: Oak Ridge National Laboratory, February 1974. Report #ORNL–NSF–EP–64, p. 11.

17. Hirst. *Energy Intensiveness*, p. 14.

18. Congressional Record Service. *Energy Facts.* Washington, D.C.: Library of Congress, 1973, p. 493.

19. Federal Energy Administration, National Energy Information Center. *Monthly Energy Review.* Washington, D.C., October, 1975, p. 20.

20. *Ibid.*, Bureau of Mines Data.

21. Hirst. *Energy Intensiveness*, p. 32.

22. *U.S. Bureau of the Census. Statistical Abstract, op. cit.* p. 512.

23. Environmental Policy Division, Congressional Research Service. *Energy—the Ultimate Resource.* Washington, D.C.: Government Prinitng Office, 1971, p. 115, Table 32.

24. Edward M. Dickson, in association with Raymond Bowers. *The Video Telephone.* New York: Praeger Publishers, 1974, p. 144.

Chapter 8

Cost-Benefit Analysis

The basic structure and communication patterns of some of the major organizational components of the insurance company that served as the subject of our case study were outlined in Chapter 3. The conclusions of that chapter were that the insurance company operations were quite suitable for decentralization through the use of telecommunications and computer technology.

Because of a set of external constraints and forces, such as the decreasing availability of an appropriate labor force in the central business district and a high clerical personnel turnover rate, the insurance company had independently decided to move its operations from the central business district to one or more less central areas to allow amelioration of these problems. However, certain constraints imposed by the national headquarters of the company upon a decentralization move acted to modify the way in which the insurance company could decentralize. Specifically, the insurance company is currently fragmenting (as defined in Chapter 2) rather than dispersing.

The following sections summarize a cost-benefit analysis for this particular company for two cases: the move actually planned by the company for 1975 and the moves that make greater use of telecommunications technology and seem to have even greater economic attractiveness.

CORPORATE DECENTRALIZATION POLICIES

In Chapter 4 a list of potential sites for dispersion of the insurance company was developed under the assumption that the primary goal of the dispersion was to reduce the employee commuting distance to the point of diminishing returns. Under this assumption a set of 18 potential centers was selected for the dispersed operations of the company. An implicit assumption in that analysis was that future employee residential distributions would be similar to the present case. However, a set of additional constraints was imposed by corporate policy of the insurance company in its selection of actual sites.

The insurance company established the following four criteria to evaluate proposed sites for the establishment of the satellites. These criteria represent minimum requirements. The responsible executives at the vice-presidential level of the insurance company believe that all four of them must be met if the proposed satellite location is to be selected.

1. An ample labor market should exist in the environs of the site, constituting a present and continuing supply of well-qualified people. This labor market should include not only recent high school graduates, but also housewives who heretofore have been unable to commute to the central business district for employment. This segment of the labor market affords the company the opportunity to establish part-time and/or flexible working hours and to obtain workers who were not previously available.

2. Suitable locations should be at least 15 but not more than 30 miles from the current centralized location.

3. Both temporary quarters and land for permanent buildings must be available at a reasonable cost. The insurance company has adopted a nationwide policy of purchasing land for its office locations and of constructing a suitable office building on the site selected. Once the site has been selected and purchased, temporary office space will be rented while a building is constructed. This will allow the insurance company to hire employees from the area and to assimilate them into the organization while construction is underway.

4. The satellite location must be able to meet equal employment opportunity requirements without incurring significant added expense or unduly distorting the company's normal employment practices. To meet this criterion, it should be possible (from the standpoints both of transportation and housing availability) for members of the existing staff to transfer to the new locations. In addition, there should be access to minority populations for new hires.

Since the insurance company plans to complete its decentralization over a period of three years, and since the primary labor pool for clerical work has been high school graduates, the current enrollment of junior high schools in the Los Angeles metropolitan area constitutes the labor market of primary interest. This consideration, the minimum satellite size constraint imposed by the national headquarters (1000 employees), and the four criteria just listed bias the potential satellite locations toward a concentration in the geographical area of Los Angeles known as the San Fernando Valley. A list of the 15 most desirable sites resulting from the analysis is given in Table 8.1. These sites were then used as the basis for developing another set of transportation cost analyses similar to those of Chapter 7.

PRIMARY DECENTRALIZATION COST ELEMENTS

Clearly, the costs of transportation are not the only considerations to be made by a firm when it is deciding whether or not to decentralize. In fact, since the employee commuting costs are only indirectly related to the cost to the company, the other costs of operation are likely to play a much greater part in the decision to decentralize. Furthermore, in the case of the insurance company, and for many companies now in the process of decentralizing from urban areas but which retain the old philosophies of corporate organization, there is an additional decentralization cost: that of personnel relocation for key employees,

Table 8.1. Potential Sites—San Fernando Valley

Site Number	Zip Code	Community
1	90290	Topanga
2	91364	Woodland Hills
3	91342	San Fernando
4	91350	Saugus
5	91304	Canoga Park
6	91324	Northridge
7	91344	San Fernando
8	91306	Canoga Park
9	91311	Chatsworth
10	91340	San Fernando
11	91302	Calabasas
12	91301	Agoura
13	91321	Newhall
14	91355	Valencia
15	91303	Canoga Park

or for all employees who wish to move, depending on the details of corporate policy. Some of these costs follow. Those categories marked with asterisks are cost elements that would not be borne or would be decreased by a company undergoing *dispersed* decentralization.

New Corporate Offices*

When it decentralizes the insurance company will establish a new headquarters office for high level executive staff in a central business district. The old headquarters building would be renovated and leased. The lease income from the old headquarters would offset some of the costs of establishing a new headquarters office and other decentralization costs. Of course, in the long term, there is the consideration of whether the available lease income would continue to increase in the CBD if decentralization becomes a popular phenomenon. However, since metropolitan populations in general tend to show a steady increase, it is anticipated that CBD occupancy will remain at a relatively high level, with the remainder of the business population increase being absorbed by growth of the regional business centers.

Personnel Relocation Expense*

This cost represents the moving expenses and the transfer allowances paid to employees and/or severance pay for personnel who are unwilling to relocate and for whom local placement within the insurance company cannot be found. For the company studied, which is undergoing in large part a "traditional" decentralization, it is estimated that there will be 1250 people involved in a reimbursed relocation to several fragmented centers for a total cost to the company of $791,000.

Training Costs*

This expense represents the costs of training of new clerks hired to replace clerical employees not accepting relocation (8% in the case studied), retraining of employees learning new jobs as a consequence of dispersion, related losses of productivity, and the time of those performing the training.

Rental Expenses*

This expense results from the additional cost of housing the satellite operations for two years until they can be moved into their permanent, company-owned quarters. For the company studied, this rental expense of $250,000 is offset by rentals received from leasing the present headquarters site. A better strategy (if it were not for corporate policy) would be to lease all decentralized office space and not to incur the expense of a corporate-owned and occupied set of buildings. This improvement results from the availability of existing office space at a lower cost than new construction. Tax considerations also clearly play a part in this decision.

Moving Expense

This category includes the cost of moving all furniture, files, and equipment from the current central business district location to the various satellite offices.

Computer Moving Expense

This represents the cost of moving the central computer to a new site in the central business district. Of course, a company would not incur this cost if it decided to retain at least a portion of the space in the building it originally occupied. But here, too, this represents an expense incurred as a consequence of other corporate policies that perceive these costs as less significant than the benefits resulting from moving the facility.

Centralized Communications Expense

This represents the cost of communication equipment at the computer site to allow a computer to operate on a time-sharing basis with remotely located satellites. The insurance company anticipates converting all its employees to operation in a time-sharing computer mode, whether or not it decentralizes. Therefore the costs of computer terminals are not included in the subsequent cost-benefit calculations, since the company will incur these costs anyway.

Planning and Contingency Expenses*

This cost represents the salaries of the planning staff required to coordinate the move and includes a contingency reserve.

Renovation and Leasing Costs*

These costs include expenses incurred in renovating the current headquarters site in the CBD and the expenses required to lease the building to new occupants.

COST-BENEFIT ANALYSIS

With these preliminary comments as background, we now present a cost-benefit analysis of the two primary alternatives.

I. Satellite offices located in the San Fernando Valley—a fragmented decentralization.

II. Satellite offices located uniformly throughout Los Angeles—a dispersed decentralization.

In the analysis that follows, all costs and benefits are compared as increments (or decrements) to the alternative of remaining in the present centralized location. That is, they are the marginal costs of operation attributable solely to decentralization.

Summary of Alternatives

Alternative I establishes a set of five office satellites in the San Fernando Valley. The insurance company (IC) has a corporate policy of owning the land and the buildings of its office operations. This means that IC will lease temporary office space to house the employees until a permanent facility can be constructed and occupied. Thus temporary office space must be rented while construction is in progress. The headquarters for the executives of the IC will be established in a central business district location. The present building will be renovated and leased. Employee separation and moving expenses must be paid, as well as the costs to establish the satellite offices. However, employee commuting costs should be less than at present, judging from the company's experience with its present satellite offices. The assumption is made that IC's productivity and staff replacement (turnover) experience with its current satellite offices continues to be valid. Thus it is expected that, once decentralization is undertaken, turnover and training costs will be less and productivity will be higher.

Alternative II establishes 17 satellite offices (in addition to the central one) dispersed throughout the Los Angeles region. By considering a larger geographical region, employee separation and moving expenses will be reduced in comparison to Alternative I (and would be eliminated, were it not for some additional factors). The same types of benefits occur in Alternative II as in Alternative I; however, the magnitudes of the benefits are different.

Additional Cost Factor Assumptions

Alternative I—Fragmentation

a. The land and building investments made by the company are assumed to have a life of 25 years.

b. The one-time expenses will be written off over a 10 year period.

c. The average compensation per employee, with all organizational levels considered, is $7500 per year.

d. The average yearly compensation for clerical employees is $6500.

e. Approximately 27% of the executives will be assigned to a central headquarters office. The remaining executives will be assigned to the San Fernando Valley.

Alternative II—Dispersion

a. A new headquarters for the executives of IC will be established in a central business district location. The present building will be renovated and leased.

b. Office space will be leased at the sites selected for office satellites. Current office rental rates in these areas were used to determine yearly office space cost.

c. IC requires a rate of return of 10% on all investments.

d. The one-time expenses associated with the decentralization will be written off over a 10 year period.

e. The average compensation per employee is the same as Alternative I, though it is possible that lower labor costs might be achieved in this alternative.

Costs—IC

A number of costs are associated with the process of decentralization and must be incurred regardless of the number of office satellites established. These costs apply to both of the alternatives and are summarized in Table 8.2. An additional training cost must be incurred in the establishment of satellite offices. Since decentralization throughout the greater Los Angeles area would require fewer new employees to be trained than would a move to the San Fernando Valley, the dispersion cost is $25,000 rather than $87,000. The cost of training

Table 8.2.   One-Time Fixed Costs of Decentralization

	One-Time Fixed Costs ($)	
	I	II
	San Fernando Valley (5 satellites)	Los Angeles Region (17 satellites)
Additional training	87,000	25,000
Additional communication	190,000	356,000
Rent	250,000	0
Moving expenses	250,000	250,000
Personnel moving/separation	791,000	50,000
Computer moving	100,000	100,000
Miscellaneous	350,000	150,000
Renovation and leasing expenses	750,000	750,000
	2,763,000	1,681,000
Annualized fixed cost (10% internal rate of return)	449,678	272,662

a new employee is estimated to be approximately $600 per person in either case.

The additional communication cost required for both alternatives is in accordance with the public utility network design discussed in Chapter 5, and consists of teleprocessing equipment and 50-kbit line charges for the computer (since the terminals are not included in either cost). A central site equipment cost of $120,000 is used, with an installation charge for the 50-kbit lines of $1900 per site. An additional equipment cost of $12,000 per satellite office is included. This is 10% of the cost estimated in Chapter 5 and represents an estimated additional cost of concentrators over and above what the company would have in its central location. As was mentioned in Chapter 5, we believe that these equipment costs are quite conservative and represent upper limits.

The rental fixed cost is $250,000 for Alternative I, since an office must be leased for a period of time until construction is completed on the office satellites. This cost does not occur for Alternative II, since IC would move directly into the leased office space. IC will have moving expenses of $250,000 in either alternative for moving office equipment to the satellite locations.

The personnel moving and separation cost is $791,000 for Alternative I, since many people who presently are employed by IC do not live in the San Fernando Valley. This cost is $50,000 for Alternative II, because the Los Angeles urban region is a much larger geographical area, and most present office employees can be reassigned to new satellite offices. There will be a certain amount of frictional placement. As a result, the $50,000 amount represents the cost of being unable to place every current employee in a suitable position, (i.e., one of the costs of residual fragmentation). This results from the necessity to have at least a minimum number of certain types of employees at some satellite locations. If a completely dispersed operation were considered feasible, this cost would not be incurred.

The cost of moving the computers and the supporting peripheral equipment is $100,000 in both cases. There is also a category of funds required for the salaries of the planning staff to coordinate the decentralization, plus a contingency reserve. Because the decentralization to the San Fernando Valley will cause more employee separation and moving expenses to be incurred than will Alternative II, this planning and contingency cost category is $350,000 for Alternative I and $150,000 for Alternative II. Table 8.2, as well as showing a detailed listing of these fixed costs, provides the annual cost based on a 10 year amortization at a 10% internal rate of return.

In addition to the one-time fixed costs, there are a number of costs that will occur each year, some of which are independent of the number of satellites. These include the operating costs of the teleprocessing equipment at the central computer and the satellite offices, the operating costs of the (leased) telecommunications lines, duplication of some administrative tasks ($50,000), and additional travel for executives ($25,000). These last two costs were estimated by executives of the insurance company.

An important consideration is the fact that if IC decentralizes, it will lose its principal office tax deduction. Under a provision of the California State Constitution, an insurance company is entitled to reduce its premium taxes by an amount equal to the property tax on its principal office maintained in the state. Only one office is eligible for this benefit. To the extent that the property tax on the present headquarters building is greater than that on the satellite with the greatest tax against it, there would be a net overall loss. The amount of this loss is estimated at $350,000. However, the California Legislature in 1975 was in the process of eliminating the principal office tax advantage. Consequently, this may not turn out to be a loss attributable to decentralization.

Benefits—IC

There are five principal benefits that will occur if IC decentralizes using either Alternative I or Alternative II.

1. Reduction in staff.

2. Reduced employee turnover and training.

3. Reduced salaries for clerical employees.

4. Elimination of the lunch program.

5. Income from lease of headquarters site.

Based on IC's past experience with its present satellite operations it can reasonably be expected that, owing to a higher caliber of applicants, a more motivated work force, and a better working environment, the productivity at the satellite offices will be higher than in the present centralized office. IC's executives believe that a 15% reduction in clerical personnel will be attainable in the San Fernando Valley decentralization (Alternative I) and a 12% reduction will occur if IC decentralizes throughout the Los Angeles urban region. This will allow IC to perform the same amount of work using fewer people thus lowering the total operating cost. Since this benefit will occur primarily at the clerical worker level, the calculations are based upon an average yearly clerical salary of $6500. It can be assumed that although the number of middle management employees required to supervise the clerical force would also be reduced, this reduction is offset by the slight supervisory duplication resulting from multiple work sites. The company currently experiences a turnover rate of 73% for first-year employees at its central headquarters and of 45% at its existing satellites. It is assumed that this 28% reduction in turnover will continue to hold. These calculations involve only the clerical employees since the only significant hiring is done at that level.

Reduced salaries (or, more realistically, reduced rates of salary increase) for clerical employees and abolition of the present free lunch program are two more benefits IC anticipates. IC believes it can continue to maintain a $10 per employee-week pay differential between the present headquarters and the satellite offices. This wage differential has been paid to attract employees to work in the central business district location. In effect, it has been a subsidy of employee transportation costs. With a decentralized satellite office configuration, employees can be hired locally, and the insurance company does not need to provide this incentive. The 1974 cost of lunches for the employees at the CBD location was $8 per employee-week.

The following calculations are based on the anticipated work force at the satellite offices, which should be 85% of the current work force for Alternative I and 88% for Alternative II. The wage differential is assumed only for the clerical employees and not for the middle or top management employees. Thus the calculations are based on the 1700 clerical employees, for whom two-week vacations, two weeks of sick leave, and 10 annual holidays are assumed.

The net annual income expected from the lease rental of the present office building is expected to be approximately $1,800,000 per year.

Cost–Benefit Comparison—IC

A summary of the costs and benefits of the two sample cases of decentralization is given in Table 8.3. There costs include the satellite operational costs just described but do not include the costs for purchase or rent of the satellite and the buildings. The net result of this partial analysis shows an annual favorable balance ranging from $3.7 million for the 18-center, areawide case, to $4.1 million for the 6-center, San Fernando Valley case, exclusive of site rental and transportation costs.

These considerations do not include any attempt to optimize the site selection process for minimum overall cost. Using the model described in Chapter 4 we have made a series of optimization calculations that minimize the site-related costs by selection of the number and location of sites. The optimization includes the cost of transportation for the employees since the company feels (and has experienced) that commuter transportation costs are reflected in salary levels. The results of the optimization analysis are shown in Table 8.4. This analysis results in two, instead of five, satellite locations being chosen for the San Fernando Valley case. For the areawide case, six satellites rather than 17 were selected. In both cases the reasons are the same: the optimum point is reached when the cost of developing an additional satellite would not be offset by an equivalent decrease in employee transportation cost.

The transportation costs are higher in Case II because it was assumed that no employee relocation would take place. Thus, although commute distances for the employees in Case II are still considerably shorter than at present, there are enough employees living at large distances (20 to 30 miles) from the dispersed centers to create size-

Table 8.3. Summary of Dollar Costs and Benefits—IC[a]

	I San Fernando Valley (5 satellites)	II Los Angeles Region (17 satellites)
Annual Costs		
Fixed costs of decentralization		
(Table 8.2)	450,000	273,000
Teleprocessing and		
telecommunications[b]	140,000	430,000
Administrative duplication	50,000	50,000
Additional executive travel	25,00	25,000
Loss of tax deduction	350,000	350,000
Total costs	1,015,000	1,128,000
Annual Benefits		
Staff reduction	1,658,000	1,326,000
Turnover and training	354,000	341,000
Reduced salaries	751,000	778,000
Lunch reduction	578,000	598,000
Income from lease of		
headquarters site	1,785,000	1,785,000
Total benefits	5,126,000	4,828,000
Benefits-costs	4,111,000	3,700,000

[a] All values rounded to nearest 1000.
[b] Operating marginal costs are estimated at $20,000 for all the system hardware, plus $24,000 for satellite offices in leased line charges.

Table 8.4. Results of the Optimization

	Alternative	
	I	II
Number of office satellites established	2	6
Fixed investment[a]	310,038	0
Variable investment	1,473,116	1,364,150
Total investment	1,783,154	1,364,150
Total transportation	665,919	1,109,740
Total investment and transportation cost	2,449,073	2,473,890

[a] In Case I, the San Fernando Valley case, the sites are owned by the company. In Case II the sites are leased at locations throughout the Los Angeles area. Thus in Case I there is a fixed investment cost which is not incurred in Case II. These sites are in addition to the one maintained near the 1974 IC location.

able transportation costs. In Case I we assumed that all employees would live a short distance from the centers. Clearly this latter method, involving employee relocation as it does, has a personal expense to the employees which is not estimated here.

Using these additional figures we can now assess the net costs and benefits of decentralization. Table 8.5 shows the results. It is clear that either case of decentralization by means of telecommuting represents a material reduction in operating costs to the company. Furthermore, decentralization over the entire Los Angeles urban region represents an additional 9% advantage in cost reduction. For the reasons stated previously the executives of the company have begun a variant of the Case I decentralization.

Employee Costs

The cost-benefit analysis from the point of view of the employees considers only the clerical employees, since middle management personnel and executives will not be affected by the lower starting salaries (although they will be affected by the elimination of the free lunch policy to the amount of $400 per year). As far as employees are concerned, the two alternatives (the San Fernando Valley and the general Los Angeles region) are ultimately equivalent because both permit working closer to where they live in the long term, if it is assumed that a local hiring policy is enforced.

IC's benefits of reduced clerical salaries and elimination of free lunches are costs to the individual employees. The average clerical employee now making $6500 per year, single, and with no other sources of income, would have state and federal income taxes reduced by $134 (1974 Tax Schedule) if pay is reduced to $5980. (Present employees would have future salary increases prestalled, rather than receiving a cut in salary.) Thus, the net annual cost of the salary reduction to the employee is $386. The lunch cost of $400 per year is an out-of-pocket expense to the employees. Hence, the total cost is $786 per year for each clerical employee.

Employee Benefits

The costs to the employees from the decentralization are, in most cases, offset by reduced transportation costs and savings in time. The minimum distance that must be saved by a clerical employee if the benefits of relocation are to exceed the cost can be determined from the following breakdown calculation for a typical employee:

annual dollar costs ($786) = annual dollar savings

$786 = transportation saving + travel time saving

$$\$786 = 2SW(C + PH)$$

where S = commuting mileage per one-way trip

W = number of working days per year

C = transportation cost per mile of commuting

P = personal cost of travel

H = average number of hours spent per commuter mile.

The factor of travel time saving is a means of placing a value on the time spent by the employee in commuting, presumably an unproductive period (although employee perceptions about this vary widely, as shown in Chapter 9). We somewhat arbitrarily placed a value on this saving of $3.00 per hour. The average speed of an urban commuter vehicle during rush hour traffic, with extensive use of a freeway system,

Table 8.5. Summary of Dollar Costs and Benefits—IC (Final)[a]

	I San Fernando Valley (2 satellites)	II Los Angeles Region (6 satellites)
Annual costs		
Fixed costs of decentralization		
(adapted from Table 8.2)	443,000	249,000
Teleprocessing and		
telecommunications	68,000	164,000
Administrative duplication	50,000	50,000
Additional travel	25,000	25,000
Loss of tax deduction	350,000	350,000
Installation costs (investment)	1,783,000	1,364,000
	2,719,000	2,202,000
Annual Benefits		
Staff reduction	1,658,000	1,326,000
Turnover and training	353,250	341,000
Reduced salaries	751,000	778,000
Lunch reduction	578,000	598,000
Income from lease of		
headquarters site	1,785,000	1,785,000
	5,126,000	4,828,000
Benefits-costs	2,407,000	2,626,000

[a] All values are rounded to nearest $1000.

was put at 30 mph. Tests by members of the research team verified this. The cost per mile figure of $0.22 is used for the IC employees since they too would pay for parking at the new sites. Thus

$$S = \frac{\$786}{2(230)(\$0.22 + \$3.00/30)}$$

That is, the break-even trip-to-work distance is 5.33 miles. Thus a typical employee saving more than about five miles per trip (approximately 85% of the present clerical staff) will receive a net benefit. An employee saving fewer miles than 5.33 will have a net cost, if the employee continues to use the private automobile for transportation. Furthermore, many of the employees, finding that they can more easily commute by other means, will reduce their transportation costs in proportion to their reduced use of the automobile.

Chapter 9

Effectiveness, Perceptions, and Attitudes

The actual and perceived effectiveness of telecommuting for each component of the information industry labor force are important elements in the telecommunications-transportation tradeoff. As noted in Chapter 1, prior research has most frequently dealt with these issues in regard to telephone, computer, and television teleconferencing at the management level. Many of the studies performed to date have concluded that a large number of management functions can be performed effectively using telephone bandwidth communications, provided that certain additional criteria are satisfied. Two of the most important criteria follow:

1.   The participants in the communication process must "know" each other, that is, be familiar with contextual clues about each other's attitudes, emotions, and so on, with the implication that face-to-face meetings must be held to some extent and occasionally repeated as a prerequisite to effective teleconferencing.

2.   Some form of contextual or graphic display must be provided. Arguments vary considerably as to the best form and/or extent of these displays. The advantages provided by standard TV capabilities do not appear to be sufficient in most cases to warrant the additional costs of the capabilities, at least for short relatively local conferences involving a small number of people [9.1].

Reid et al. have also performed extensive studies on management perceptions of the effectiveness of telecommunications as a substitute for travel [9.2]. Reid found that management level personnel, at least those without extensive prior experience in teleconferencing, felt more confident about their decision-making abilities in face-to-face settings than in a teleconferencing mode, even though there were no substantial differences in judgments made in the latter mode.

Since our study emphasized applications of telecommunications at the clerical level, the research team was concerned with both the effectiveness of telecommunications use at this level and the perceptions of potential users of a telecommunications system. Unfortunately, few data on these two elements are available in the public domain, and the conditions of our study did not allow us to make measurements of effectiveness or an extensive examination of the attitudes of the clerical staff at the insurance company.

It should be pointed out that this scenario for substituting communications for transportation assumes that the individual worker will be performing essentially the same tasks now being conducted, is currently engaged in a task and occupation that is amenable to remote communications, and works in an industry in which efficiencies may be gained (e.g., insurance). While telecommunication–transportation substitutes may make sense in terms of tangible cost-benefits, it is entirely a separate matter to measure whether or not telecommunications substitutes for transportation make sense for the organization in terms of total impact, including intangible cost-benefits, and whether they make sense for the individual to willingly adapt to the new telecommunications substitutes. Our data and others' indicate people do in many cases like to travel, people do in some cases prefer to commute, and people in many cases prefer to "get out of the house." Finally, bear in mind the organization provides a significant social function for the individual; for many people the organization is their sole people-meeting place and provides their major friendship network.

RESISTANCE TO INNOVATION–IMPLEMENTATION

The innovation diffusion literature [9.3] suggests that innovations diffused top-down through the hierarchy are more apt to be resisted, disadopted, and/or sabotaged compared to innovations diffused collectively. Acceptance of an innovation by an individual in an organization is dependent upon a number of factors.

1. The norms in the organization for innovation, whether supportive or rejecting.

2. The extent to which the communication loops in the organization are open and allow the entry of feedback about innovations.

3. The extent to which the innovation is compatible with existing methods.

4. The extent to which an innovation has a perceived relative advantage.

5. The extent to which an innovation is easily understood and not complex.

6. The extent to which the innovation may be tried on a small scale.

Although many of the variables just discussed are related to the nature of the individual, the one most critical item relates to norms of the organization in which the diffusion occurs.

Data [9.4] we gathered in major United States corporations presently involved with implementing automated tradeoff systems suggest that if an executive goes into an organization and suddenly informs a subordinate supervisor that in the future his or her employees will not be performing their tasks interdependently and collectively in the office but rather from remote distributed work centers, he is apt to meet with considerable resistance. Aside from the fact that the employees were not consulted or at least made part of the innovation decision-making process, the supervisor will be threatened because apparently his or her empire is being diminished. The employees are also being threatened because their peer networks are suddenly broken up, and they are faced with establishing new work habits associated with adjusting to new work environments.

In addition, the employees probably suspect that via telecommunications their performance and productivity rates are objectively measurable across any unit of time. Also, telecommunications substitutes for transportation that do not involve remote data transmission or teleconferencing and are literally a one-for-one functional task substitute will require retraining of personnel. The retraining situation is threatening, as reeducation tends to be, and may also create union and pay scale problems. Finally, the employees may be threatened by the mystique of the computer, a phenomenon still highly persuasive among "older" personnel, particularly those with nontechnical backgrounds.

Organizational Impact

Consider the transition period of an existing organization that decentralizes. One characteristic that is significantly affected is the informal communication network within the organization. It supports the friendship and peer groups as well as the morale of the organization and generally functions to keep productivity up. Overlaying a telecommunications network on an informal network, which itself cuts across the formal (task) networks, increases the potential for employee resistance to the tradeoff by disrupting their habits, friendships, and psychological sets. The eventual reconfiguration of these networks will initially affect productivity and morale unless the transition is planned cooperatively with the employees and supervisors and provides little surprise to the participants.

In a negative sense the boredom, lack of interaction, and disruption caused by adoption of poorly designed telecommunications substitutes could significantly affect the productivity and turnover rates of the organization for quite some time. For example, one insurance company in the Midwest has had to pay a premium to hourly workers in order to keep turnover rates acceptable after conversion to an automated, distributed data processing work mode. However, a positive feature for the organization is that it will be better able to gauge productivity and hence set competitive pay scales within occupational categories.

Perceptual Evaluation

To assess effectiveness and attitudes of one type of tradeoff, the research team designed a series of surveys of users of related telecommunications substitutes to assess attitudes toward telecommunications both before and after experience with an existing system. Also, a general survey was taken of a random sample of the Los Angeles general adult population to gather data on public knowledge of and attitudes toward the various types and potential uses of telecommunications. A similar set of surveys were conducted with USC evening and day students who did not have experience with any telecommunications systems except conventional television, radio, and telephone.

INTERACTIVE INSTRUCTIONAL TELEVISION

Some frequent mention is made in the following section of the Interactive Instructional Television systems (IITV) at USC and Stanford University. A brief description of these systems is in order. The USC IITV system, established in 1972, is designed primarily to serve professionals in engineering, aerospace, and information sciences who wish to take graduate level courses. These students are generally in midcareer and usually are employed full-time by industries located from 10 to 30 miles from campus. Before installation of the IITV system, some of the students commuted to the USC campus either in the evening or on a released time basis during the day. Others who became IITV students did not previously take courses at all because of the inconvenience of commuting.

The IITV system transmits live and videotaped lectures, at microwave frequencies, to 12 regional centers from the studio at the University of Southern California. Ten of these centers are located in the offices of major companies in the Los Angeles metropolitan area; two sites are in regional business centers and service clusters of companies. Regular academic courses are offered, both credit and noncredit, graduate and undergraduate. Since the program started an average of 40 courses per semester have been offered by USC over the IITV network. The system includes a voice-only talkback capability provided by FM radio transmitters at the remote sites. Special equipment is required at each site to receive the course broadcasts and to transmit students' questions. A daily courier service delivers and picks up homework, exams, and other class material.

To join the network, a company installs the specialized television equipment, provides classrooms, and pays a participation fee based upon the total number of employees at the site. The cost of equipment depends on whether a one-room or a multiple-room system is established. Equipment may be either leased or purchased. Although in some cases the company pays tuition fees, most students pay their own regular tuition fees plus a surcharge for the privilege of "telecommuting" via the IITV system. The surcharge is generally greater than the student's out-of-pocket commuting costs, even allowing for appropriate personal income tax deductions. The Stanford University system is essentially identical in concept, although older and more extensive, and was included to provide a more generalizable sample population for the surveys.

SURVEYS

A series of five surveys was designed and conducted to obtain information about attitudes toward the telecommunications-transportation substitution. The following populations were surveyed:

1. An areawide random probability sample of Los Angeles County adult residents. The sample was interviewed via telephone and yielded 197 respondents.

2. A sample of the USC population of Interactive Instructional Television students enrolled in remote classrooms at their place of employment. Questionnaires were administered in person. These subjects, like their Stanford University counterparts (see below) were primarily professionals in engineering, aerospace, and information sciences, taking graduate level instruction during released time.

3. A sample of Interactive Instructional Television students enrolled at Stanford University. The sample has similar characteristics to the USC group. Respondents mailed in their answers to USC.

4. A comparable group of night USC commuter students who were seeking advanced degrees in engineering. In some cases these stu-

Table 9.1. Survey Factors

Predictive and Descriptive Factors	Dependent Factors
IITV Factors[a]	IITV Attitudes (Scaled)
Enrollment status	Effectiveness
Instructor evaluation	Affinity
Purpose of enrollment	Aid to job
Enrollment consequences	Aid to career
	Aid to productivity
Local Transportation Behavior	
Number of automobiles	Transportations Attitudes
Travel time	(Scaled Evaluations)
Travel distance	Purpose
Mode of commuting	Relationship to job
Behavior during commuting	Relationship to home neighborhood
	Duration
Innovativeness/Rigidity	Travel interlude
Five item innovativeness scale	
	Value and Desirability of
Use and Perception of	Telecommunications Services
Telecommunications	Interest in and amount
Use of television	willing to pay for:
Use of radio	Educational delivery
Use of telephone	Pay entertainment
Use of touchtone	Telemedicine
Use of CATV	Electronic funds transfer
Use of other media	Civic function access
	Video conferencing
	Facsimile
	Library data banks
	Self-improvement services
	Remote job linking

Table 9.1.   *Continued*

Variables[b]	
Predictive and Descriptive Factors	Dependent Factors
Long Distance Business Travel	
Amount	
Purpose	
Substitution potential	
Nonbusiness adjuncts	
Demographics	
Sex	
Age	
Income	
Housing	
Education	
Marital Status	

[a] Not pertinent to L.A. County Sample
[b] The variables were organized into clusters of predictor and dependent factors. Measurement was made by means of closed categories on questionnaires, except for those items eliciting personal evaluations. The following factors are common to all studies.

dents also had the option to enroll in Instructional Television classes during the day. In other instances lack of access to the IITV system precluded its use.

5.   A sample of regular daytime undergraduate students enrolled at USC. Because of the urban setting of the USC campus (near the primary Los Angeles CBD) and consequent commuting by most students, students were sampled as to their attitudes toward electronic delivery of education.

In summarizing the results of the surveys, the populations are divided into users and nonusers. The first category includes only the IITV students at USC and Stanford University. The second category includes the Los Angeles County general population sample, the USC night students, and the USC undergraduate students.

Because the IITV system is television-based it provides a different set of communication modalities from the computer-based systems which have been the main subject of previous chapters. It allows some modes of visual and aural communication which are not available on a computer-mediated system, while making other modes (e.g., data look-up, text editing) more difficult. In spite of these differences, the team anticipated that the attitudes of the users toward the IITV systems might not be materially different than the attitudes of clerical trainees toward a computer terminal system.

A series of variables were identified that were common to all the surveys. These variables were organized into clusters of predictive and dependent factors. Measurement was made by means of closed categories on questionnaires, except for those items eliciting personal evaluations. The factors are detailed in Table 9.1. A more detailed discussion of methodology may be obtained in a related report [9.5].

Users: IITV Students

The members of this group are characterized primarily by their use of a wide-band telecommuting system. Their attitudes toward the system were measured at the beginning of the academic semester and then later in the semester after several months of system use. The two groups, USC and Stanford, showed little variance in attitudes; therefore, they are discussed as one group except in those instances where notable differences in attitude were detected. There were no significant control group differences to merit covariance procedures.

The average round trip commuting distance for the IITV users (when they commuted from work to campus) was 17 miles. This figure is slightly below the national average commute to work distance of 18.8 miles. The pie diagrams in Figure 9.1 illustrate the attitudes of the IITV students toward IITV and commuting, respectively. The phrases used in the survey follow (code words were not underlined in the survey—they are underlined here only for clarification).

IITV	Commuting
1. Participation in IITV will eventually help my *career*.	1. Commuting is a *necessary evil*.
2. IITV *helps* me do my *job* better.	2. Commuting is a *useful interlude* between home and school.
3. Time spent with IITV takes away from my on-the-job *productivity*.	3. I spend *too much time* commuting.
4. IITV is as *effective* for me as in-the-classroom education.	4. I *need* to commute in order to *live* where I live.
5. I *like* IITV *better* now than last month.	5. I commute in order to *have* the *job* that I have.

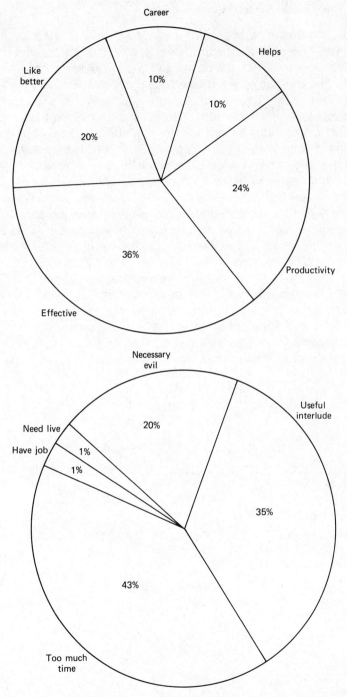

Figure 9.1 (a) Attitudes toward IITV; (b) attitudes toward commuting.

Table 9.2 illustrates pre- and post-telecommuting attitudes toward commuting based on two factors: one an evaluative factor, the other a pragmatic factor based on home and job considerations. The data indicate that the subjects remained fairly constant in their evaluation of the IITV system. The exceptions are item 4, which shows a trend toward greater affinity over time, particularly by USC participants, and item 1, which indicates a trend toward greater resentment of on-the-job time spent with IITV by USC participants but less resentment by Stanford participants. It should be noted, however, that this may be partially attributable to differences in course work as a function of the different university curricula. Further analysis of the data indicated that subjects (55%) tended to feel that they were not missing something of importance on campus by enrolling in the IITV program. Most (60%) felt their attitudes toward IITV would become more positive in the face of a continued energy crisis. With respect to this latter point, it should be noted that the first series of surveys were conducted prior to November 1973, and it may be postulated that broad attitudinal changes toward commuting and transportation in general may have occurred as a result of the "energy crisis" of late 1973 and early 1974.

Respondents were also asked evaluative questions concerning the IITV system, specifically, what improvements they would make. The

Table 9.2.   Pre-and Postattitudes toward Telecommuting

		Pre		Post	
		USC (%)	Stanford (%)	USC (%)	Stanford (%)
1. Time spent with IITV takes away from my on-the-job productivity	Agree Disagree	43 57	69 31	77 23	45 55
2. Participation in IITV will eventually help my career.	Agree Disagree	95 5	97 3	100 0	94 6
3. IITV is as effective for me as in-the-classroom education	Agree Disagree	63 37	65 35	63 37	61 39
4. I like IITV better now than last month	Agree Disagree	36 64	52 48	60 40	57 43
5. IITV helps me do my job better.	Agree Disagree	86 14	77 23	86 14	84 16

USC group primarily suggested improved audio/video technology, whereas the Stanford participants preferred improved administrative functions (courier service). The Stanford group also indicated a need for improved video. Both groups wanted better material presentation by the instructors (a desire not necessarily confined to the IITV system). Tables 9.3 and 9.4 illustrate student attitudes toward various facets of IITV technology enhancement. Greater importance was placed on two-way audio interaction and delayed replay features. However, using dollar estimation, students indicated they would be willing to pay greatest dollar amounts for better television resolution (for clearer presentation of written and graphical material), instant playback, and interruption capability.

The conclusion that may be reached from these two sets of data is that students using the IITV systems desire better detail and audio/visual manipulation features that have yet to be developed in most applications of video-telecommunications, with the exception of some specialized 1000-line resolution telemedicine systems. We did not

Table 9.3. Desirability of Technology[a]

	USC IITV	Stanford IITV
Two-way talkback	4.5	3.6
Delayed replay	4.7	4.3
Color	2.5	2.3
Classroom scanning	3.0	2.4

[a] Scales ranged from extremely unimportant (1) to extremely important (5). The higher the value, the more important.

Table 9.4. Value of IITV Technology[a]

	USC Undergraduates	USC Evening Students
Interruption capability	6.84	4.10
Instant playback	9.04	3.95
Split screen	2.86	1.05
Better audio and stereo	3.05	1.79
Color	4.92	2.24
Real-time transmission	3.71	2.19
Student control of camera	3.04	1.85
Better resolution	18.07	4.94

[a] Average amount extra, per television credit, the student would be willing to pay (in dollars) for items.

examine the issue of whether provision of the alphanumeric display features of a conventional computer terminal, complemented by a facsimile printer with high resolution (both using telephone lines) would satisfy this desire. Additionally, these responses indicate that students strongly favor some form of control that is analogous to hand raising in the classroom.

The following conclusions may be drawn from the survey of the IITV students at Stanford and USC:

1.   Instructional television as a telecommunications substitute for transportation offers the IITV user a substantial savings in time and travel. The director of the IITV system at USC, Dr. Jack Munushian, estimated that in its first two years of operation, the USC IITV system saved 250,000 commuter miles [9.6].

2.   One of the major motivations for participation is a willingness on the part of the participant to complete or expand his or her educational training; given this motivation, the convenience and ease of the IITV system play a major part in the decision to participate. A corollary to this conclusion is that IITV students tend to feel that the availability of the system resulted in their taking a more aggressive attitude toward continuing their education; some students attended IITV courses who would not otherwise take them.

3.   Users of an IITV system show greater affinity over time, indicating that familiarity with the system can favorably affect attitudes toward the system.

4.   Over 60% of the participants perceived IITV as being as effective as in-the-classroom education (with Stanford students showing a slight decrease in this assessment over time). Comparison of grades and performance ratings by the instructors indicated essentially identical academic achievement for participants in the two modes (IITV and in-the-classroom). This response indicated that no appreciable (or at least quantifiable) loss in effectiveness was occurring as a result of using the IITV system. In fact, in a pilot program run at Stanford students at one IITV site were considered to be below the general capability of students attending on campus. They were given the same courses as on-campus students and were also allowed to review videotapes of the courses, under the guidance of an on-site tutor (a fellow employee who had already taken the course). Their performance was superior to that of the better-qualified, on-campus students. Stanford is considering expansion of this tape-tutor capability.

An independent and less extensive survey of the USC IITV participants was conducted by the Administrative Assistant at the USC IITV
Center. This survey supported the conclusion that the availability of
the system resulted in a more aggressive attitude toward continuing
education, primarily because it was easier to take the necessary
courses. The survey also indicated that convenience was a key factor, with most students indicating that time saved was highly important
to them and that use of the system minimized time loss from work and
disruption of family life. Finally, the survey indicated that 50% were
willing to pay the cost of driving their car for the IITV service and
24% were willing to pay 50% more than the cost of operating their
car for the IITV service.

Nonuser Populations

The nonuser surveys were designed to assess the attitudes of "naive"
populations (i.e., people who are unfamiliar with computer and advanced communications technologies) toward telecommunications as
a substitute for transportation. The objective was to get some estimate
of the predisposition of the entry level information industry workers
toward, or against, telecommuting. The sampled populations in this
group include: (a) undergraduate daytime students at USC (some of
whom commute from neighborhoods throughout Los Angeles and
some of whom live on the campus), (b) part-time night students at
USC who had had no experience with the IITV system and who commuted to the school to attend classes, and (c) a random sample of the
general adult population of Los Angeles county.

Transportation Patterns.   Analysis of the nonusers' transportation patterns showed that their commuting behavior was comparable to that of
the user populations (Table 9.5). The average round trip commute for
the Los Angeles random sample population was 19 miles (the same as
the national average in metropolitan areas), as compared with 16 for
the IITV students and 17 for USC night students. The USC day student
commute to school was shorter, at 13 miles. However, the combined
time commuting to work and school of the employed day students and
part-time night students varied from 10 to 45% more than the time
spent commuting by Los Angeles general population and from 30 to
70% more than the time spent by the IITV population.

Nonuser Attitudes toward IITV.   Of the nonuser population the undergraduate daytime students, who traveled the most, were the least receptive to alternate forms of educational delivery. The primary reason

Table 9.5. Respondent Commuting Behavior

	L.A. Random Sample to Work	IITV–USC to Work	IITV–Stanford to Work	USC Night Students to Campus	USC Day Students to Campus
Average round trip time from home to work or campus	46 min.	39	39	33	29
Average round trip distance	19 miles	16	16	17	13
Average number of cars have access to	1.2 cars	2	1.7	1.5	1.5
Round trip *time* from campus to work	NA	NA	NA	33	21
Round trip *distance* from campus to work	NA	NA	NA	21	11

for preferring to commute to campus was a preference for the campus environment and the interaction permitted by that environment. A second reason for a negative response toward IITV was that the character and allowable hours of work of the employed students was not amenable to this form of educational delivery, suggesting that undergraduates who are employed primarily in part-time, nonprofessional work, would have difficulty in having access to IITV as it is currently offered.

The part-time evening students, who had the highest average commuting distance of all the groups sampled (17 miles round trip to work and 21 miles from campus to work), were more receptive to IITV, with 36% indicating that they would use IITV at work and 46% indicating they would use IITV at home. Those who gave a negative response cited, again, a preference for the campus environment and interaction with others on the campus.

The Los Angeles County random sample showed that job considerations were an important element in the decision to commute, with 86% agreeing that they needed to commute in order to have the job they had. Commuting was seen as a necessary evil by 68% of the population sampled, but only 32% felt they spent too much time commuting.

Responses to questions on their attitudes toward telecommunications substitutes for transportation to their jobs indicated the following:

- L.A. respondents were generally evenly split about their willingness to work closer to home via telecommunications links.
- Those respondents most receptive to dispersion tended to commute the greatest amount, perceived their time as being more important than those who were not receptive to dispersion, and exhibited a mild degree of dogmatism.
- Most respondents preferred working closer to their home but not in it.
- The majority would pay nothing additional per month for this privilege, perceiving dispersion as a fiscal responsibility of their employers.
- Overall attitudes toward commuting were positive or showed acceptance of commuting as a necessary evil. The data indicate that other considerations dictate commuting habits to the extent that people would rather give up their residential location than their job to decrease their commuting. It was difficult to convey the idea in a short interview that they could change their job location without changing their employer.
- Commuting is perceived along at least two dimensions: an evalu-

ative factor of affinity and demand; a pragmatic factor of home and job considerations. These two factors are not strongly related.

It should also be noted that the Los Angeles population was relatively unaware of various telecommunications modes and alternate uses of those modes. For example, although 9% of the general population had cable television, 14% did not know what cable television was, and 33% more did not know if it was available to them. The indications that close to half of those surveyed showed no interest in cable has significant implications for cable television's growth rate and, consequently, the development of in-the-home services via cable. It clearly indicates need for education of the public about cable; it may also indicate the need for cable franchisees to develop additional services that would attract those nonsubscribers who already have adequate television reception.

It is interesting to note that 17% of the general Los Angeles sample reported possessing touchtone telephones—almost double the cable television penetration figure. Since the touchtone is complementary to future interactive telecommunications, the market for telecommunications services may lie with this group. We must assume, of course, that those paying the additional $1.00 per month touchtone surcharge (Los Angeles rates charged by General Telephone and Electric, and AT&T) would also be willing to pay the basic cable rate.

Attitudes toward Future Technology Services: Users and Nonusers

Tables 9.6 and 9.7 detail the perceived value of and interest in a variety of home telecommunications applications. Respondents were asked to estimate a dollar value they would willingly pay (in addition to a cable television charge) for such services and also to indicate (rank) which services they would purchase if they were available now. (Appendix 2 defines the categories of services listed below.)

It is interesting to note that the dollar evaluation of telecommunications services by the Los Angeles County population and the USC undergraduate population is much more generous than the IITV populations. The USC team attributed this difference to the fact that the IITV populations have had experience with the technology and are involved in engineering-related disciplines. Consequently the IITV populations may have a greater sense of the "true" value of the delivery of such services.

Table 9.7 shows that there are differences between value and desirability ranks of future telecommunications services, so that edu-

Table 9.6. Ranks of the Value and Desirability of Telecommunications Services[a]

	Value			Desirability		
	L.A.	IITV	USC	L.A.	IITV	USC
Course credit	1	1	2	2	9	2
Shopping	6	4	7	9	7	7
Entertainment	4	2	3	1	2	1
Medical	3	3	1	5	4	6
Banking	9	10	10	10	8	9
Government functions	8	11	9	6	3	8
Visit friends	5	5	4	3	5+	3
Facsimile	11	9	8	8	10	8+
Data bank	10	7	5	7	5+	5
Self-improvement	7	8	6	4	1	4
Job from home	2	1 USC 6 Stanford	[b]	11	6	[b]
Visual access	[b]	[b]	7	[b]	[b]	8+

[a] The L.A. Population rates entertainment as most desirable, but would pay most per month for course credit.
[b] Not asked.

cational services, vocational links, telemedicine, pay-television entertainment are most valued among the Los Angeles population. However, the Stanford group ranks vocational links well below cable shopping in dollar value, perhaps because of the better environmental conditions, lower housing density, and easier commuting in the Palo Alto area.

In terms of immediate purchase behavior, however, home entertainment, educational services, video conferencing with friends are ranked as being most desirable by the Los Angeles general population and the USC undergraduates, while the IITV samples rate hobby services, home entertainment, civic functions as being most immediately desirable. The difference in this latter sample is again partially attributable to the fact that they are already enrolled in instructional television at their job location and do not perceive an additional need.

In a factor analysis of the data from the Los Angeles County sample two telecommunications factors emerged that elucidate some of the above findings. The first major factor explaining the variance of this group's perceptions of telecommunications is one in which the values of educational services, banking, entertainment, and civic func-

Table 9.7. Value and Desirability of Telecommunication Services

		L.A. Population	USC and Stanford IITV Participants	USC Under-graduates
Course credit	Price[a]	16.37	8.60	11.77
	Rank	2	9	2
Shopping	Price	7.75	3.70	4.33
	Rank	9	7	7
Home entertainment	Price	11.29	4.85	9.27
	Rank	1	2	1
Medical	Price	13.19	4.15	23.33
	Rank	5	4	6
Home banking	Price	3.43	1.55	2.94
	Rank	10	8	9
Government functions	Price	5.90	0.72	3.01
	Rank	6	3	8
Video conferencing	Price	9.47	3.40	7.21
	Rank	3	5	3
Facsimile print	Price	2.55	1.90	3.15
	Rank	8	10	8
Databank	Price	3.06	2.20	5.17
	Rank	7	5	5
Self-improvement/ hobby	Price	6.07	2.00	4.62
	Rank	4	1	4
Job from home	Price	15.07	9.74–3.11	[b]
	Rank	11	6	[b]
Visual access and scan of print media	Price	[b]	[b]	3.69
	Rank	[b]	[b]	8

[a] All prices are in additional dollars per month the respondents would be willing to pay for the services (aside from basic cable costs).
[b] Not asked.

tions cluster together. This tends to indicate that respondents generally evaluate these services along the same underlying dimension, grouping together those services that are more passive, that is, less interactive. When coupled with the desirability data (above) *the first*

*factor indicates that the greatest potential for marketing telecommuni-
cations (without additional consumer education) is found among "survival" oriented information services.*

A second, relatively pure telecommunications factor comprises evaluation of video conferencing, access to data banks, self-improvement
services, facsimile printing, and home occupational linking. This factor
might be labeled the personal role definition factor, which tends to
involve primarily interactive services that are supplementary to "survival."

These data suggest that while individuals will pay more for services
perceived as more complex (telemedicine and vocational linking),
desirability of the services is not related to dollar value. The data
further indicate the following:

- There is a market for supplementary educational telecommunications services that would permit people to take refresher courses
and high school and college curricula for credit.
- There exists a market for "pay" television delivery of high quality
entertainment not available currently.
- That the underlying motivation for use and acceptance of such
services relates to social function and perceived passivity (factor
one) or activity (factor two) of user involvement.

Since most individuals do not comprehend or desire remote vocational linking (at least in the home), policy and perhaps costs will
need to be mandated by the organizations involved. Of course, people
like to "get out of the house" and may not have the room or privacy
to work remotely at home.

Nevertheless, a number of individuals are apparently willing to pay
for home vocational linking today. There is no motivational reason
why, in the near future, more organizations could not encourage the
use of phone-coupled computer terminals by personnel who can work
with relative task isolation (e.g., computer scientists, finance specialists,
and secretary/typists).

Conclusions

Some overall conclusions related to the development of telecommunications-transportation tradeoff policy are warranted by the survey.

Instructional Television Tradeoffs

- Instructional television, as one manifestation of such a tradeoff, offers the participants a substantial savings in time and travel.

- Even though one of the major motivations for students to participate is the desire to complete or refresh their education, convenience and ease play a major part in their decision to make the telecommunications-transportation tradeoff.
- There is a substantial market for home educational delivery, both among part-time students and the general adult population.
- Most respondents are willing to pay the equivalent cost of driving and maintaining their automobiles for such a service.

Local Transportation Behavior and Occupational Networking

- Commuting is evaluated primarily along a time and tolerance dimension and a separate, more pragmatic dimension of relationship to home and occupational environment.
- Occupational stability considerations are more important than others in influencing commuting, in that people would rather move than change jobs (under the assumption their jobs are immobile) if they want to affect their commuting patterns.
- The general adult population (51%) would prefer not to work from their homes, but would work in neighborhood areas closer to home. Most would not pay anything additional for the opportunity to work closer to home, hence making it the responsibility of their employer.

Perception and Use of Telecommunications Services

- A substantially greater percent of the population possesses touchtone telephone service than subscribes to cable television; the touchtone telephone service is a readily available technological supplement that is complementary to future technological services.
- Adults evaluated educational services, vocational linking, telemedicine, and pay television higher than other potential telecommunications services; however, they would immediately purchase, were the services available, pay television entertainment, educational services, and video conferencing services.
- The underlying motivation for the use and acceptance of such services relates to social function and the perceived passivity of the man-telecommunications interaction; a second dimension is perceived man-telecommunications activity.

In conclusion, the surveys indicated that the general public does not really fully comprehend the potential or operation of pending telecommunication .developments. These data also indicate that, while individuals are receptive to many telecommunications substitutes, they are not yet ready to fully accept, by a slight margin (51%), remote occupational networking. Of those who are amenable, however, the model of a neighborhood center for remote telecommunication "offices" appears to be the most acceptable.

REFERENCES

1. Anna E. Casey Stahmer and M. Dean Havron. *Planning Research in Teleconference Systems.* HSR–RR–73/10–St–X. McLean: Human Sciences Research, Inc., September, 1973.

2. Communications Studies Group, Joint Unit for Planning Research. *Miscellaneous papers submitted to the Steering Committee by the Experimental Research Team: February 1971 to May 1971.* Ref: P/71135/CH. London: University College London, May, 1971.

3. G. Hanneman and W. McEwen, Eds. *Communication and Behavior.* Reading: Addison-Wesley, 1975. See in this book "Structured Communication" (introduction), pp. 185–196; W. McEwen, "Communication, Innovation and Change," pp. 197–217; and E. Rogers and R. Agarwala-Rogers, "Organizational Communication," pp. 218–236.

4. G. Hanneman and W. Spindell. *Human Factors in Automated Information Systems.* Final Report. Los Angeles: University of Southern California, Annenberg School of Communication, July, 1974.

5. Gerhard J. Hanneman. *Consumer Attitudes and Perceptions About Telecommunictaions Substitutes for Transportation: Final Report.* Los Angeles: University of Southern California, Annenberg School of Communications, 1974.

6. Jack Munushian. "USC's Interactive Instructional Television System Expected to Eliminate a Million Commuter Miles Annually by 1975." News release. Los Angeles: University of Southern California, January, 1974.

Chapter 10

Other Tradeoffs and Direct Impacts

To this point we have been discussing one particular aspect of tele-communications alternatives to transportation. We have focused on the use of telecommunications to decrease commuting, because this appears to have the greatest single potential for near-term economic and energy impact. However, there are several other areas in which telecommunications may be a suitable alternative to transportation. Brief descriptions of these tradeoff situations follow.

BUSINESS TRAVEL—LOCAL

In addition to the enormous amount of travel devoted to commuting to work, there is a significant amount of travel performed during business hours primarily related to information transfer of one form or another. Roughly 10% of intraurban automobile travel is associated with business activities other than the commute to work. About half of the intercity travel in the United States is related to business. Furthermore, business uses of intercity modes of transportation tend to be concentrated on the more energy-intensive modes, such as jet aircraft, which according to Hirst, equal the urban automobile in energy cost per passenger mile [10.1]. Thus, this general, noncommuting business travel appears to have great potential for substitution by telecommunications technologies.

However, it is vital to note that the information transfer processes that are completed by these forms of business travel are by no means the same as those accomplished by the routine commute to work. Businessmen travel to make sales, to engage in various forms of management conferences, and to attend conventions. Interpersonal social communications play an important part in each of these purposes. Consequently, the extent to which telecommunications can substitute for transportation in these cases is probably considerably less than in the commute-to-work situation.

As mentioned in earlier chapters, some of the major barriers to the use of telecommunications for sales and business conferencing are found in the attitudes of management-level personnel that the use of telecommunications would not be as effective as the holding of a face-to-face meeting. Quite often the expense and general lack of availability of a video teleconferencing system is given as a major reason for not using telecommunications (the assumption being that television might be an effective surrogate but that nonvideo forms of telecommunications are definitely not as effective). However, the various experimental tests of teleconferencing reviewed in the Appendix indicate that in most cases video conferencing has no advantage over the various audio forms of teleconferencing. In fact, in some cases video and face-to-face conferences were felt to be less effective than audio teleconferencing where the desirability of the impersonality provided by an audio teleconferencing link is considered to be a significant factor. Furthermore, participants in audio teleconferences tend to spend less time in desultory social discussion, concentrating more rapidly on the business point of the conference.

To provide an anecdotal example of this phenomenon we note that during the course of the first year of its activities the USC Research Team held a series of meetings with executives of a major national telephone company, whose offices were some 18 miles from the USC campus. The round trip travel time from the campus to the telephone company was slightly more than an hour. Observance of the social amenities, on the average, occupied 10 to 20 minutes of each visit, with total visit length ranging from 1 to 1½ hours. Two initial meetings were held in this manner, with the research team traveling to the telephone company offices.

The meetings had two primary purposes: (1) to set up the necessary agreements for exchange of information, and (2) to establish personal relationships with the various executives involved. Subsequent meetings were carried out primarily by a telephone conferencing system in which campus operators patched in phone lines from the offices of various members of the research team, while a similar process occurred at the telephone company offices. During these meetings, requiring no travel time, the social amenities occupied less than a minute, and the business transactions generally required less than 20 minutes.

A key adjunct to this conference procedure was the documentation

(data requirements, network descriptions, etc.) that had to be transferred between the two groups. This was sent ahead by mail, timed
to arrive a day before the scheduled teleconference. This method also
helped focus the discussions and keep them short. However, even this
documentation could have been transmitted by interactive computer
techniques if the telephone company offices had been equipped with
terminals.

From the evidence gathered to date it appears that 20 to 60% of
local business transportation could be replaced by properly planned
telecommunications. As with telecommuting, increasing costs of transportation or increasing threat of the unavailability of gasoline will begin
to cause more organizations to adopt various modes of teleconferencing for their ordinary business purposes.

BUSINESS TRAVEL—INTERCITY

Roughly half of all intercity trips by air are made for business purposes and presumably involve communications transactions at management levels. Consequently, it is instructive to examine the relative
costs of travel by air to distant cities and compare them with the
costs of attending teleconferences involving two or more people. We
assume the conferees are using a computer-mediated conferencing
system, augmented by an audio telephone capability, and some means
for facsimile reproduction of graphic material. This combination is used
because, from the evidence already discussed, it appears to provide
all the communications capabilities required for many types of business meeting.

The cost of travel time includes, for our illustration, the costs of
airline tickets, time spent in travel, and overnight accommodations.
In order to increase conservatism in our estimates, we do not include
the cost of meals or the costs of local transportation to the meeting
place or between hotels and restaurants. The cost of teleconferencing
includes the marginal cost of operating the necessary equipment for
the duration of the teleconference, and the cost of operating the long
distance transmission line between the two locations. Furthermore,
two different types of transmission between the two locations are
assumed: the standard common carrier service provided by AT&T
and a specialized common carrier service, as exemplified by the
EXECUNET Service of MCI Telecommunications. These costs are compared in Table 10.1. The table generally indicates that teleconferencing has a cost advantage over travel, an advantage that increases with

Table 10.1. Long Distance Communication Costs from Los Angeles

Terminus	Duration of Conference	Travel[b]	Costs[a] Telecommunications[c] Common Carrier	Common Carrier Specialized
New York	1 day	473.23	225.21	189.09
	2 days	498.23	450.42	378.18
	3 days	523.23	675.63	567.26
Chicago	1 day	370.53	214.94	178.82
	2 days	395.53	429.88	357.63
	3 days	420.53	644.82	536.45
San Francisco	2 hours	72.50	53.70	Service
	4 hours	72.50	117.19	not
	8 hours	72.50	234.38	available
	2 days	97.50	449.16	

[a] Costs are estimated for January 1, 1976, and include all applicable taxes.
[b] Air travel cost includes the following: coach round trip air fare, cost of flight time plus 1.5 hours travel to and from terminal, at $11.00 per hour, and lodging (for New York and Chicago only) at $25.00 per night, with the number of nights equal to the number of days.
[c] Telecommunications costs include an effective lease rate of $2.45 per hour for a CRT terminal with conference (speaker) phone and a facsimile machine (all time-sharing the line). The common carrier is assumed to be the Bell Telephone System. Daytime, station-to-station rates were assumed. The specialized common carrier is assumed to be MCI Telecommunications, using its EXECUNET service, which is available from any push-button telephone in the cities served.

the distance between the two cities. It also shows that the specialized common carriers have a price advantage over AT&T for the period considered. For short haul travel (i.e., trips less than 500 miles), teleconferencing has a cost advantage only for relatively short conferences.

There tends to be a certain amount of over conservatism in Table 10.1. For example, even though a business conference may nominally be said to continue for an entire day, the actual communications interchange often takes only a fraction of that time. As mentioned earlier, the transactions in a teleconference tend to be more rapid than in a face-to-face conference. For these reasons the actual costs of teleconferences in typical business situations may be substantially less than those presented in the table. Further, a value added network, such as the TELENET system which uses packet network switching, charges by the amount of information transmitted, rather than by the time spent connected. This could effect an additional saving over the example presented in Table 10.1. Finally, the teleconference has one important advantage over a face-to-face conference in that its scheduling is much more flexible. A conference can occur almost on the spur-of-the-moment. In an asynchronous teleconference, even this last requirement need not be met, and the conference can occur at any local time, day or night.

The data communications satellite provides additional scope to the potential for intercity teleconferencing. By essentially eliminating travel delays on a global scale, it permits international networking of present business and governmental communication and allows many new communications functions to be performed that would otherwise be entirely impractical [10.4]. Here, as in the less global cases already mentioned, asynchrony is vital to effective operation of the system.

HEALTH CARE DELIVERY

There has been considerable interest over the past decade in investigating the uses of telecommunications, particularly video telecommunications, in improving the delivery of health care services. An excellent general overview of the topic of "telemedicine" is provided in a report by Ben Park, entitled, "An Introduction to Telemedicine" [10.4]. Telemedicine, in Park's sense, is confined to the use of two-way, interactive television for various health care transactions.

In general, telemedicine systems used in the course of examination, diagnosis, and/or treatment of a patient are most effective when competent nursing or paramedical personnel are available at the site where the patient is located to carry out the "attending" physician's instructions. Clearly, where a television system of high technological quality is used, all the visual and aural cues to a patient's condition are available to the physician, who may be located at some considerable distance from the patient. The key features in patient examination that are not available over a telemedicine system are those involving palpation (that is, feeling the patient for the presence of such symptoms as abnormal skin temperature, moisture changes, or resiliency of tissue). Teleoperators (that is, mechanical surrogates for hands and fingers which may be remotely controlled by the physician) have not progressed to the point where they can serve as useful substitutes for a physician's hands. However, in many cases, nurses and paramedical personnel can perform these functions effectively. If these allied medical personnel are available at the patient's side most of the remote diagnosis and treatment functions, in principle, can be effectively served by telemedicine systems. However, the experience to date has also shown that the present cost and unwieldiness of video systems tend to discourage their use for providing health care delivery in remote areas, especially when the system cost must be borne entirely by private hospitals [10.5].

Aside from the uses of video telecommunications, however, there are a number of important areas in which audio bandwidth data transmission functions can be quite important. These functions tend to fall into two general categories: The first is the ability to gain access to centrally located data bases to obtain patient histories, to interact with computer-assisted diagnosis programs, or to acquire specific information about various medical facts and issues. In any of these cases the physician has access to information that may be physically located in a computer file thousands of miles from his own location.

The second type of nonvideo interaction can involve such things as consultation with other physicians (perhaps using the transmission of graphic information such as X-rays—possibly processed by computer image enhancement techniques), supervision of allied medical personnel, monitoring of nonvisual patient information (such as EKG signals), and the use of various forms of training systems and devices.

A lack of research at this point leaves considerable uncertainty as to whether these uses of telecommunications in health care will have significant effects on transportation use. In terms of the impact on the national level, the effect is likely to be quite small. However, the impact of various telecommunications systems on the productivity of physicians and allied health care personnel may be quite significant, since the time that ordinarily would be spent in transporting these personnel can now be made available for the health care functions themselves. Similarly, patients who would otherwise have no timely access to medical personnel can be treated through use of these techniques. This is extremely critical in emergency health situations and in remote areas.

EDUCATION

Some examples of the uses of interactive instructional television (IITV) systems have already been presented in earlier chapters. The feature that appears to be of the greatest importance in educational telecommunications systems is the interactive capability. That is, the ability of the student to ask questions during lectures, thereby clarifying his or her perceptions of the material being presented, is a main determinant in the learning process. As we have learned from experience with the USC and Stanford IITV systems, it is not necessary that this return communications link in the interactive system provide video information. In fact, as mentioned earlier, it may well be unnecessary to use television in the transmitted lectures if adequate means for displaying graphic material can be provided.

Here, as well as in the business environment, the ability to use narrower bandwidths for transmission of information may be significant. For example, the USC IITV System occupies all four channels available in the Los Angeles area. There is no more spectrum space for additional channels operated either by USC or by other educational institutions. This situation is not uncommon in metropolitan areas in the United States. In practice, then, most educational institutions interested in providing telecommunications-enabled off-campus instruction, must either use commercial VHF or UHF broadcast television or telephone networks of some sort. The use of broadcast television generally confines the student to courses delivered in the early morning hours. Telephone networks are considered deficient because of their general inability to transmit graphic information at economic rates with presently available facsimile equipment (although this area of the equipment market is developing rapidly). As in the other aspects of the tradeoff, the issue hinges on the relative costs of transmitting educational information via telecommunications versus the cost of transporting the students to a central educational site.

In remote areas such as the outback of Australia telecommunications techniques have been considered for years to be quite effective in providing educational services. Radio techniques were developed there because of the prohibitive time and money costs of transportation. India, Brazil, and Iran are experimenting with satellite broadcasting of educational programs as the only feasible means for providing these services to remote areas. In urban areas, however, the transition to cost effectiveness will come only when inexpensive means for nonbroadcast transmission of information are available, such as the intercenter network hypothesized for the insurance company in Chapter 5.

There has been much discussion among educators of the possibilities for interactive cable television (CATV) systems as a means for expanding the availability of education for those who cannot go to the central facility. However, contemporary interactive CATV systems have extremely limited useful bandwidth. Most "two-way" cable systems, even at the experimental stage in 1975, do not allow for voice response channels from each customer in the system. The reason for this limitation is the cost of providing a system with sufficient electronic sophistication to allow an identifiable verbal request to be made by any one of several thousand potential viewers. Consequently in education as well as in business operations a dispersed system, which concentrates response points, appears to be the most economically attractive alternative, using presently available technologies.

DELIVERY OF GOVERNMENT SERVICES

In 1974 the Annenberg School of Communications at USC engaged in a study of the requirements for two-way telecommunication systems for the delivery of various municipal services [10.6]. The requirements research led to the identification of two primary areas in which it appeared that there could be significant impact on the productivity of municipal service delivery. Two types of telecommunications systems were postulated, one for each area of service delivery.

1. *An electronic public counter* for providing two-way, interactive audio and graphic communications for enhancement of city and county job-seeking, screening, counseling, interviewing, and placement functions for many decentralized neighborhood locations. The postulated system incorporated expansion capabilities for additional services that would require individual negotiations and transactions between individual citizens and decision making authorities.

2. *A community video conference facility* for providing simultaneous and immediate two-way audio-visual interaction between several citizen groups located throughout a community and the city planner, with expansion capabilities for additional local government decision making activities requiring broad citizen participation.

These recommendations focus on two major problems in the provision of municipal services. Both of them are closely coupled with problems of transportation. The first problem was to develop and disseminate a central, current data base concerning the availability of jobs within the municipal government. At a later date the data base could be expanded to include jobs anywhere within the metropolitan area. The job information would be available to prospective employees at a number of sites scattered throughout the metropolitan region. More important, city personnel at the remote sites would be able to provide preliminary screening of the employees and to arrange for interviews with prospective employers, all in a single transaction. Since the computer-stored data base would be frequently revised (at least once a week), job information would be timely, and much of the frustration experienced by job seekers presumably would be significantly reduced.

Without such a telecommunications system job seekers are forced to travel to several different locations in order to get job information. Quite often the information is inaccurate or obsolete. After a series of unproductive encounters with the system, many job seekers become disenchanted or hostile. Thus, aside from elimination of transportation costs for job seekers, it appeared that the employment information system would have positive social benefits because of its effective use of telecommunications.

The purpose of the video teleconferencing system was to allow large groups of interested citizens to interact more effectively in various city processes, notably city and regional planning. In this system two-way video conferencing was to be implemented allowing city planners to present their current plans for various regions of the city and use the fairly extensive information and display available in the centrally located planning office. The planners would teleconfer with citizen groups assembled at mini-city halls in the urban regions involved to discuss various elements of the overall city plan. As in the case of the municipal public counter segment, the teleconferencing system would follow a dispersed design similar to that outlined in Chapter 5.

In both the electronic public counter system (operating at audio bandwidths), and the video conferencing system (operating at video bandwidths), the perceived advantages to the city officials concerned and to the affected citizenry were not primarily those of reduction of transportation. The primary advantages were seen to be in their ability to provide services not effectively delivered by other means.

THE TELECOMMUNICATIONS, COMPUTER, AND TRANSPORTATION INDUSTRIES

Clearly the telecommunications-transportation tradeoff directly affects the economies of these major sectors of U.S. industry. Increasing use of telecommunications will have a related but not necessarily identical effect on the uses of transportation. In fact, Cowan argues that transportation and telecommunications are directly interrelated; as the use of one increases, so does the use of the other [10.7]. The general reason given for this is that the extension of man's horizons and contacts through the uses of telecommunications increases the desire to travel to the places contacted for purposes of tourism or business. This increase in travel is said to parallel the increase in telecommunications used.

In telecommuting, however, these considerations are not applicable to the clerical and related personnel who may comprise much of the telecommuting work force. Furthermore, other restrictions on uses of travel, particularly diminished availability of fossil fuel, further serve to reduce the use of transportation relative to telecommunications.

A development instrumental to increased interurban telecommuting is the formation of the specialized and value-added common carrier networks. A specialized common carrier is one that provides telecommunications transmission channels between its various offices located in principal urban areas. For example, MCI Corporation, the first of the specialized common carriers to begin operation, has a private data network that served 40 cities in 1975. The services offered by the specialized carriers range from a combination of voice, data, facsimile, and teleprinter services in the case of MCI, to the data-only services offered by Datran.

Each of these specialized common carriers employs a private microwave transmission system interconnecting clients in the cities served by means of central offices in each city which contain the necessary computer and transmission equipment. A user of one of the specialized common carriers typically "calls" the nearest office of the carrier via the telephone system and begins his conversation, or connects his terminal, through the carrier network to the message recipient in another city. The advantage to the user of a specialized common carrier, as was illustrated in Table 10.1, is that the rates charged for data transmission are generally less than those charged for the same data by the more conventional common carriers, such as members of the Bell System.

The value-added carrier differs from the specialized common carriers and private data networks in that it adds data manipulation technologies, such as packet switching, which tends to increase the response flexibility and reliability of the data transmission.

Both of these types of network have come into existence only in the last few years and, in some cases, only in the last few months. Consequently, it is too early to develop quantitative information, either on their impact on telecommuting or of the impact of intercity telecommuting on the carriers. Nevertheless, they represent an important new trend in this process.

Although these new types of network have been discussed primarily as they relate to internal use in the United States, it is easy to envision their extension, through communications satellites, to an international scale. This extension of reach of the data networks compounds the impacts in every area discussed in this book.

CONSUMER AND SMALL BUSINESS SERVICES

Telecommunications technologies already play a significant role in reducing the use of transportation for provision of consumer services. Effective use of the telephone to check on the availability of goods and services at local stores constitutes a way of life for many citizens. The use of telecommunications for increasing the availability of special services, such as accounting and payroll preparation services for small businesses, extension of library systems with computerized data bases, the resurgence of the ability to order goods by telephone, all point to a steadily increasing use of telecommunications instead of transportation. For many of these services, the primary decision criterion for the consumer is not the money it costs to travel to the various business establishments offering the goods or services. The more important consideration is the time lost in performing the travel, especially when several visits must be made in a single day.

Cable television systems have pointed to the use of such systems for purposes such as remote shopping as a major new extension beyond their primary present use for delivery of entertainment. However, not enough experimentation has been performed to date for accurate predictions to be made concerning the extent to which consumers will prefer the advantages of interactive cable systems in speeding up the shopping process, over the possible disadvantages of not being able to physically examine the goods prior to purchase. Another consumer-perceived disadvantage is expressed in the fear of becoming financially overextended because it is too easy to purchase goods using such a system.

PRIVACY AND SECURITY

A ubiquitous concern in the use of telecommunications systems is the often-justified fear that conversations are being "overheard" by unauthorized persons. The reactions to this potential compromise of the integrity of messages transmitted over telecommunications systems vary widely. The insurance company we studied seemed relatively unconcerned about the possibility that its data transmissions might be intercepted by others. At the other end of the spectrum, the U.S. Department of Defense spends many millions of dollars annually in research and development designed to encrypt or disguise data transmissions so as to minimize their chances of interception or proper interpretation.

The Federal Privacy Act, which went into effect in 1975, places specific strictures upon the development of centralized data bases and the uses and accessibility of information derived from them. As we have already mentioned, the problem of maintaining the integrity of data concerning financial transactions has been a major stumbling block in the development of electronic funds transfer systems.

About the only conclusion we can reach at this stage is that, since the cost of transmission security increases proportionally with the level of security required, those organizations that are not highly concerned with security issues are more likely to adopt telecommuting before those that are more concerned with the protection of routine operating information.

A great deal of protection of information can be achieved without the need for elaborate security precautions. For example, within the insurance company, information concerning policyholders can be protected simply by referencing all information transmitted to the policy number (or application number), rather than to the name of the policyholder. Since information concerning policies is generally transmitted only in a fragmented way, it is unlikely that any electronic eavesdropper on the telecommunications lines interconnecting the satellite offices of a dispersed insurance company would be able to collect coherent information on any one policyholder without enormous effort and expense.

In other respects the privacy or, more exactly, the impersonality of the telecommunications process is considered by many individuals and organizations, in many situations, to be a definite advantage over a face-to-face conversation. In fact, the intrusive capability of the private telephone coupled with its transmission privacy (when a speakerphone is not used) allows a caller the ability to interrupt face-to-face meetings—an ability that often allows relatively trivial telephone messages to penetrate important face-to-face discussions. Similar situations can be imagined when the computer terminal replaces the telephone: a face-to-face meeting can be enhanced as one of the parties to the conversation uses a CRT terminal at his or her desk to query a data base to provide additional information to supplement the content of the conversation. Similarly, the appearance upon the nearby terminal of a message for one of the participants in a conversation can as easily disrupt that conversation as would a ringing telephone.

TECHNOLOGICAL FACTORS

The discussion thus far has been concerned primarily with the effects of existing, commercially available telecommunications and computational technologies. In several cases where telecommunications substitutions for transportation are feasible in principle the cost of the substitution is presently too high or the effectiveness is too low to warrant a choice in favor of telecommunications on the part of the prospective user. Some technological developments that can be expected to have major influence on both cost and effectiveness include the following:

1. *Development of Fiber Optics Systems.* Because of their ability to accommodate transmission bandwidths that are enormously higher than those available with microwave cable, fiber optics promises to constitute a major factor in the development of telecommunications capacity, particularly in areas that already have a near-saturation level of telecommunications traffic (or, as in the case of New York City, where there is said to be no more room under the streets for more wires). This will be true especially when fiber optics transmission lines can be used for long-distance communications, since presently the transmission costs are the major component of long-distance telecommunications costs.

2. *Computer Terminals.* Two areas in the development of computer terminals will affect the rate at which these increasingly useful devices diffuse throughout our economy. First, as computer technologies continue to advance, the costs of computer terminals for a given level of capability will continue to decrease. Correspondingly the degree of flexibility and sophistication of terminals at a given price will increase. Both of these trends will broaden the market for the terminals— ultimately to the point where they are as ubiquitous as television sets.

The second advancement in the technology will be the development of hybrid terminals and data processing systems that will allow easy transmission of data and voice information over the same link. This terminal will be of particular value in many of the teleconferencing systems previously described, where neither voice nor data transmission alone are sufficient to satisfy the purposes of a teleconference, but where the combination of the two in an effective way may do so. In order for such terminals to be effective, a companion development is required to allow digital encoding of voice signals and yet provide realistic reproduction. Another factor required in the development of hybrid terminals is the capability to provide graphic display of information not easily delivered in either voice of alphanumeric form. At present this industry is quite reminiscent of the high fidelity audio industry of 20 years ago in that a few scattered components of each description are available, but no well-integrated systems exist as yet.

REFERENCES

1. Eric Hirst. *Energy Intensiveness of Passenger and Freight Transport Modes, 1950–1970.* Report #ORNL–NSF–EP–44. Oak Ridge: Oak Ridge National Laboratory, April, 1973, p. 21.

2. Edward M. Dixon. *The Video Telephone.* New York: Praeger Publishers, 1974, Chapter 10.

3. Robert H. Kupperman, Richard H. Wilcox, and Harvey A. Smith. "Crisis Management: Some Opportunities." *Science,* Vol. 187, February 7, 1975, pp. 404–410.
   This article points out the utility of international computer telecommunications networks as a means for averting military conflicts and similar international crises. The common use by representatives of various nations of a "central" computerized socioeconomic model is postulated as a way of developing mutual understanding—and resolution—of international tensions.

4. Ben Park. *An Introduction to Telemedicine.* New York: New York University, the Alternate Center, School of the Arts, June, 1974.

5. Jon D. Wempner, M.D. *Telemedicine: An Initial Experience.* Proceedings of the National Telecommunications Conference, NTC 1974 Record. San Diego, December, 1974, pp. 206 ff.

6. Gerhard J. Hanneman and Herbert S. Dordick. *Implementing Two Urban Telecommunications Experiments Designed to Deliver Municipal Services.* Los Angeles: University of Southern California, Annenberg School of Communications, Center for Communications Policy Research, January, 1975.
   This reference was simultaneously a report of an experiment definition study funded by the National Science Foundation and a proposal for two demonstration experiments. Although enthusiastically endorsed by officials of the City of Los Angeles, the proposed experiments were not funded.

7. Peter Cowan. "Moving Information Instead of Mass: Transportation Versus Communications." In *Communications Technology and Social Policy.* George Gerbner, Larry P. Gross, and William H. Melody, Eds. New York: Wiley-Interscience, 1973.

Chapter 11

Indirect Impacts

There is a considerable and varied body of literature dealing with the probable impacts of computer and telecommunications technologies on society. At the extreme end of the scale are such fictionalized projections as E. M. Forster's *The Machine Stops* and George Orwell's *1984*. At the other end of the scale are detailed discussions of particular technologies, their individual merits, and special applications. In between these two extremes lies a body of literature that summarizes, debates, ponders, postulates, and/or advocates, depending on the author and the particular aspect of the subject under consideration.

Within the last decade a new field of public policy-related research has developed, called Technology Assessment. The basic objective of the technology assessment process is to anticipate the probable effects on society of a newly developing technology and to provide policy recommendations that would lead toward maximizing the benefits available from the technology while minimizing its harmful effects or disbenefits. This field of research has grown to the extent where there is now an Office of Technology Assessment serving the United States Congress which, together with the National Science Foundation, funds or performs a variety of assessments of the potential impacts of developing technologies upon society. (For example, the National Science Foundation announced in June, 1974, that it would fund a technology assessment of the interaction between telecommunications and transportation. The contract for the assessment was awarded to the Stanford Research Institute.)

A technology assessment distinguishes between two types of impacts produced by a technology. The first comprises the direct impacts. These are specifically those effects that the introduction of the technology was originally intended to create. The second comprises the secondary or indirect impacts of the technology. These are the societal, environmental, and other effects that occur because of the existence and use of the technology, even though the technology may not directly affect them. This chapter and parts of previous chapters, taken together, constitute a preliminary technology assessment—preliminary in the sense that detailed information on the scope and magnitude of many of the potential secondary impacts does not exist at the time of writing this book.

In recent years various scholars have undertaken studies of the direct impacts of telecommunications–transportation tradeoff. The most pertinent of these already have been referenced and are summarized in the Appendix. The main thrust of many of these studies and of the preceeding portions of this book has been that telecommunications probably can be used to replace, supplement, or provide alternative means of performing a variety of functions: transportation to downtown business organizations; transportation to campuses or intercampus travel; intracity, intercity, and international business travel; delivery of urban government services, recreation, and cultural events into suburban and rural areas; delivery of various medical services in both urban and rural areas; opening of job markets to the handicapped; and so on.

More fundamentally, however, the idea of viewing telecommunications as an alternative to transportation raises profound questions about the indirect impacts of this alternative and about the innate structure of American society. Over the past few decades we have come to accept transportation, particularly automobile transportation, as integral to the way of life enjoyed by most Americans. The wide availability and use of individually owned and driven automobiles has been a primary factor in the creation of urban sprawl, development of freeways, static or declining use of mass transit, growth of urban air pollution (and of government agencies to fight it), deterioration of central metropolitan areas, inefficient use of transportation energy by urban dwellers, rush hour traffic congestion, the formation of almost single use central business and separate residential districts, and so on. The automobile and auto parts sales alone account for 17% of retail sales in the United States [11.1]. At the same time the widespread availability and use of individually owned automobiles have also permitted increased job mobility, expanded use of recreational areas, high employment in critical sectors of the economy, the development of mass production technologies, the development of single-family housing developments outside our cities, and rapid, flexible transportation for most Americans.

Until the early 1970s the United States' economy was operating as if expansion of the automobile industry and increasing dependence on the automobile were destined to be continued indefinitely. However, the well-documented but heretofore poorly acknowledged fact that the oil reserves of the world are finite has begun to cause widespread reevaluation of this concept at all levels of the economy. The key immediate influences in this reevaluation were the Arab oil embargo, which highlighted our dependence on oil, and the consequent "energy crisis" of 1973–1974. As a result of the recognition on the part of public policymakers of the limitations on our petroleum resources, we are now at a decision point as a society; we must decide whether the way of life made possible by the automobile since the turn of the century will (or can) continue, or if we should consider alternate or modified modes of working, communicating, and living.

Our reliance upon transportation is traditional. It is an accepted belief and custom that *going* to work is a prerequisite to being able to perform that work. We are now entering an era in which technology permits us to communicate between distant points and to perform certain kinds of work in places far removed from the place where that work will be used or stored. We are also in an era where transportation is primarily oil dependent, despite the limited and declining supply of oil. These two observations alone, without further elaboration, should encourage us to consider alternatives and to formulate new approaches to the ways and patterns of our daily lives. To facilitate informed public policy decisions, the spectra of "problems" and "solutions" must be clearly understood and ranked in terms of their severity and national utility, respectively. Since Americans tend to think in terms of problems and solutions, a transportation problem list would include the following:

- Declining availability of petroleum.
- National dependence on foreign oil and the associated problems of increasing trade deficits.
- Transportation-related pollution.
- Costs of building and maintaining highways.
- Increased costs of automobile manufacture and operation.
- Urban sprawl as a result of white-collar migration from the cities and the concomitant decline of the inner cities.
- Loss of time, property, and lives from automobile accidents.

Solutions that have occupied much public attention in the last few years include reallocation of fuel resources by

- Development of nuclear, solar, and/or coal energy to replace petroleum, making it more available for transportation use.

- Strip mining of the western states to develop oil shale reserves.
- Development of nonfossil automobile fuels (such as hydrogen, methanol, batteries, etc.).

Other solutions might include reduction of transportation energy use by the following:

- Increased use of telecommunications and computer technologies.
- Reduced oil consumption through rationing or conservation.
- Development of mass transit.
- Modified automobile engine design.
- Combinations of the foregoing.

Viewed in this context telecommunications and computer technologies become an option—an option that permits greater flexibility in defining our national priorities. City, state, and federal decision makers should become aware of the possibilities and problems inherent in that option and should formulate public policies to mitigate possible adverse effects and to maximize possible beneficial impacts of the telecommunications option.

Based on the findings of our research, we feel that current communications and computer technology is sufficiently advanced and diverse to be an economically feasible alternative for transportation in certain industries—the information industries in particular. Furthermore, communications and computer technologies have the potential for acting as catalysts that could radically change the structure of American society in much the same way that the automobile acted as a catalyst on our way of life during the first half of this century.

For example, consider the possible impacts of telecommunications on the most general level. At least the following areas could be affected by a widespread utilization of telecommunications and computer technologies:

- Organizational structure, management methods.
- Urban structure and land use.
- Availability and use of natural resources, energy in particular.
- Environmental quality.
- Transportation system structures, components, and modes.
- Working conditions and patterns of business interaction.
- Educational systems.
- Government policy efficiency.
- Information industry productivity.
- International relations.
- Telecommunications and transportation industry growth.

- Labor policies and practices.
- Employment patterns.
- Technological development.
- Family structure.

All the above areas are integral to American life. They are molded to some extent by our national reliance on the automobile; it is reasonable to expect that telecommunications, if used to provide an alternative to transportation, could have a comparable influence in many or all of these areas. The areas of greatest secondary impact are discussed more fully below.

TRANSPORTATION

Present and planned mass transit systems and freeways are strongly influenced in their design, their routes, and their service levels by the assumed need to transport day workers to and from the central business district, and by the anticipated steady increase in this need as population increases. As a consequence, these systems are either hopelessly overcrowded and inefficient during the peak hours (because the commuter population has increased faster than anticipated), greatly underutilized during the off-peak hours, or both. Furthermore, our urban freeway systems and central business districts are generally reaching capacity; many major cities frequently voice a pressing need for new or modern rapid transit systems.

The present system is caught in a spiral of trying to match the ever-increasing demands. Two problems predominate. First, the cost of new systems is high, because of the high costs of obtaining new rights-of-way and of the perceived need to overdesign the average capacity of the system in order to accommodate the peak commuter loads. Second, new transit systems generally require combinations of municipal bond issues, federal grants, and new taxes to finance the massive new capital investments. Public resistance to this trend is demonstrated by the repeated and continuing defeat of these bond and tax issues in most U.S. cities. The financial difficulties experienced by New York City may have increased the resistance of investors to purchase of municipal bonds at their usually lower rates. Even the infusion of 18 billion dollars of federal mass transit subsidy, which was voted by the U.S. Congress in 1975, appears insufficient to provide adequate mass transit to major urban areas in the near future.

Because of the substantial and rising costs of building and operating such systems, telecommunications would seem to present a viable and logical alternative. Telecommunications could alleviate the need for constant expansion of the transportation system(s) through permitting development of a dispersed network of work centers throughout the urban area, linked by telecommunications. If workers could travel shorter distances to local office centers, localized transit systems could be used which would be less costly and more easily developed than major fixed-rail or similar conurbationwide systems. These systems would involve buses or personal rapid transit which, because of the short hauls involved, could be lighter, smaller, and less energy consuming than today's standard buses. People could still use freeways and line-haul transit systems for shopping, cultural, and sports events, and for activities that might be located at other nodes around the city. New line-haul systems, if needed, would connect nodes at the periphery and could be more easily optimized for the average traffic load rather than for the disappearing commuter peaks.

Conversion to telecommuting would be a gradual process which would not require massive new public capital investments. At the very least, large urban areas that are presently under intense pressure to commit money to the development of transit systems primarily geared to commuter transportation could have considerably more flexibility in the allocation of city, county, state, and federal monies if telecommunications were to be used more broadly as a substitute for transportation.

URBAN DEVELOPMENT

A set of conflicting forces can be anticipated in the area of land use planning as a consequence of increased use of telecommunications. On the one hand, greater concentrations of growth—regional activity centers or nodes—within the metropolitan areas are foreseeable and are growing in favor with urban planners. On the other hand, increased urban sprawl can be an equally likely possibility, given the increased locational flexibility afforded by telecommunications. In principle, almost no locational constraints are put upon an individual or organization wishing to work by means of telecommuting.

Our research foresees evolution of the existing urban structure into a new form of community or communities. In particular, a possible step is the "rural city," which mixes the familiar downtown business area and urban living, with the result that central business districts would no longer be predominately single use in their design. Instead of monolithic structures devoted solely to office use, new high-rise building clusters may evolve with a mixed selection of offices, living quarters, parks, and entertainment facilities. City dwellers could enjoy some advantages of small town living in that they could live and work in the same general area; at the same time, they could enjoy the cultural advantages and activities of a major metropolitan area.

As has been mentioned in earlier chapters, many city planners are now tending toward the development of the types of urban structures just described. Although relatively new to the United States this trend in cluster development has been underway for some time in Scandinavia. For example, several regional centers of this sort surround Stockholm. As was the case for the insurance company in our case study, we find that many factors independent of telecommunications are forcing cities to focus more attention toward cluster designs and development of new towns with multiuse buildings of the sort just described. Columbia, Maryland, and Reston, Virginia, are examples of these suburban regional centers.

Yet from both of these there is now considerable commuter traffic to Washington, D.C., the center of the conurbation containing Columbia and Reston. Hence, the new urban developments, which inherently have the ability to reduce commuting by allowing people to live and work close to their homes are, in fact, increasing it because the traditional commuter patterns are still being maintained. Nevertheless, as the costs of commuting increase, as major highway or freeway developments continue to be curtailed or cancelled, and as the cost of single-family dwellings continues to rise above the means of the average family we anticipate that greater attention will be paid to the telecommunications alternative as the enabling link in this trend of development. Thus telecommunications will provide the final locational freedom to supplant and augment that formerly offered solely through transportation.

As with all cases of increasing freedom of choice, however, we must begin to consider the possibility that freedom may become license —the urban growth equivalent of the "tragedy of the commons" [11.2]. For example, one of the potential results of the greater locational flexibility provided by improved and less expensive telecommunications technologies is that people will move to areas of great scenic beauty or recreational potential in such numbers as to destroy the resource they moved to be near. The choices are to risk the destruction of such major natural resources, through our typically inadequate planning for this possibility or, through careful planning, to provide alternative scenic and recreational areas in cities. We may have to combine limitations with access to our extraurban resources in order to conserve them. It seems possible that as people spend more time living their entire days in suburban areas, they may take more care in providing parklands in these areas, thus avoiding the urban monotony so typical of U.S. cities.

It should be noted that these descriptions are of possible, not necessarily probable, urban futures. Land use and development codes currently are primarily local, or at best regional, concerns. To date, city planners have generally oriented (or zoning boards have allowed) city developments around a central business district. In recent years the business centers have become surrounded by rings of slurbs—slums and abandoned buildings. This has been caused largely by the transportation-enabled flight of wealthier inhabitants to the suburbs. As a consequence the problems of revitalization of decaying central city areas have become significant.

Considerable amounts of money and effort have gone into urban renewal programs (most of which have been only partially successful) and the introduction of improved transportation facilities and systems into the central areas. As indicated earlier, new rail rapid transit systems are being planned throughout the country, most of which are designed to increase the centralization of the cities by moving people, primarily commuters, downtown more efficiently. The momentum of this new downtown planning movement is great. Within a few years city planners will have to reexamine this concept in light of the new telecommunications technologies or they will lock themselves into the present pattern. The policy recommendations of city planners and decisions by city governments are particularly crucial since the constraints on and the impacts of decentralization are numerous in several critical areas, including zoning laws, taxation, design of municipal service delivery systems, location of public buildings, and so on.

ENERGY

One of the major impacts of the substitution of telecommunications for transportation is in the area of energy conservation. This has already been covered in Chapter 7.

A secondary aspect of this method of energy conservation is that a substitution of telecommunications technologies for transportation would induce a proportionate change in the requirements for the type of delivered energy from gasoline to electricity. Hence, one of the higher order impacts to be considered is the effect of telecommuting on the demand for increased supplies of electrical energy. There is also a retroeffect of the impact on the speed of acceptance of telecommunications substitutes. This is caused by the inevitable delays in adding new electrical power plants in an urban area. Since it presently takes about eight years from the initial decision by an electric utility to build until initial operation of a conventional electrical power plant, and up to 12 years or more for development of a nuclear power plant, some attention must be paid to the dynamics of interaction between these related technologies. Since power systems are regulated by government bodies at state, regional, and federal levels, it is apparent that government energy policies are critical if adequate electrical energy supplies are to be available.

ENVIRONMENT AND RESOURCE MANAGEMENT

Telecommuting clearly reduces energy use where it substitutes for transportation. It also requires a different form of delivered energy than that required for most forms of transportation. Both of these immediate impacts have further consequences in environmental pollution. For example, urban automobile traffic constitutes approximately 80% or more of the contribution to urban air pollution. It would appear that for each 1% reduction in urban automobile traffic brought about by conversion to telecommuting, a reduction in urban air pollution of approximately 0.8% would result. In fact, the reduction may be even greater.

One of the reasons for this is the fact that much of the air pollution caused by automobiles occurs during acceleration, deceleration, and idling of the automobiles. In turn, these processes occur more frequently during the hours of peak traffic and accompanying congestion. Consequently the use of the automobile for commuting tends to be more responsible for urban air pollution than do other uses of the automobile [11.3].

The 20% of urban air pollution not contributed by the automobile comes generally from stationary sources, some of which are fossil fuel supplied power plants. However, these power plants can generally operate with pollution controls that are more efficient than those in the process of being installed on automobiles. Consequently, the diversion of telecommuters from automobile operation to use of electricity will probably have a negligible effect on the air pollution component from stationary sources.

Finally, the removal of automobiles from the existing road and highway systems will allow the systems to operate at points closer to their most efficient capacity during the rush hour periods that still remain. This improved traffic flow will in itself improve the operating efficiency of the automobiles, reducing both their specific energy consumption and their contribution to air pollution.

Widespread development of telecommuting can also have effects on our use of primary resources. For example, the United States already has a sizeable fraction of the world's copper resources invested in the form of transmission lines for telecommunications systems such as the telephone. Greatly expanded use of telecommunications could create serious resource extraction problems if suitable materials to substitute for copper were not produced.

One means of reducing the copper use for telecommunications channels is to convert from the use of separate twisted pair conductors for each line to multiplexed channels transmitted over a coaxial cable. For this solution to be feasible, the length of the twisted pair lines (which must be used to distribute the individual channels to telephones or computer terminals from the termination of the coaxial cable) must be kept quite short. This is not feasible if these lines must go to an array of physically dispersed houses or other buildings. Thus we have another reason for a dispersed form of decentralization rather than for the modern-day equivalent of the cottage industry implied by the ultimate form of diffusion decentralization.

Ultimately the development of efficient, low-loss, fiber optics transmission lines may provide the answer to this problem. These transmission lines are composed primarily of quartz, a very abundant mineral resource. Thus they promise an enormous leap not only in basic data transmission capability, but in greatly increased decentralization flexibility and in minimized impact on metal resources.

Similar resource use tradeoffs must be considered. In the comparison between telecommunications and transportation, we see that automobiles, trains, buses, and rails use enormous quantities of iron. On the other hand, they do not use the rare earth metals that are used in computers and telecommunications equipment. The typical automobile has one or more tons of mineral resources embodied within it, whereas the typical computer terminal and associated computational and data transmission equipment may have only 100 pounds of resources invested in it. Yet, the resources used in manufacture of the computer terminal are often considerably less abundant than those used for the manufacture of the automobile. These issues can be resolved only after detailed comparisons of resource use for each of these alternatives have been made. We have not yet made this comparison.

LABOR RESOURCES AND WORKING CONDITIONS

Decentralization by means of telecommunications offers opportunities for new work styles that are not based on the 40-hour, 9 to 5 workweek. Labor resources can be made available to organizations that are not available to them now. This latter factor was one of the main reasons for decentralization of the insurance company we studied. In that case the motivation of the company was to move closer to sources of qualified high school graduates who would form the company's full-time clerical staff. The company was also becoming interested in the idea of attracting part-time staff comprising housewives and students. These factors are likely to be attractive to many other information industry firms as well.

A worry frequently expressed by information industry managers who are considering decentralization, and particularly dispersion, is the fear of inadequate supervision of clerical employees. As was mentioned in earlier chapters, it is quite feasible, particularly in cases where the tasks are relatively routine, to develop computer software that can allow continuous and objective tests of the performance of each employee. For instance, test case transactions can be presented to the employee, mixed in with his or her normal work load. The employee's responses to the test example, as monitored by the computer system, can provide an accurate means for testing his or her reliability of response on the rest of the work load. It is entirely possible that more objective measures of employee performance and productivity can be made by this means than may be available through the traditional supervisor-employee relationship.

This issue must be treated with considerable care, since it can appear quite threatening to both employee and manager. The employee can feel spied upon and intimidated by the invisible computer, and the supervisor can easily develop fears of his position being usurped. On the other hand the existence of an objective, computer-based measure of work performance, which is essentially independent of the conditions at any particular work site or time, can allow workers to perform their jobs in locations and at times most convenient to them. Therefore a company wishing to adopt these means of assisting supervision should treat them as a way of increasing working flexibility and work satisfaction, rather than as the more threatening means of keeping a more careful eye on its employees.

A related problem for the aspiring executive in a dispersed work center is that he or she may feel that promotional opportunities are more restricted because of decreased face-to-face contact with higher management. Since the feasibility of objective, computer-mediated testing of performance diminishes as the level of management increases, the aspiring manager may indeed be more dependent on performance evaluations that require the more subtle means of communication available through more frequent face-to-face contact.

From the individual employee's point of view, strictly mechanistic telecommunications substitutes for transportation can adversely affect him or her in the following ways:

1. By making job productivity objectively measurable (quantifiable), some subtle, nonobjective performance indicators may be lost.

2. Expressions of source credibility can become strictly quantitatively measurable. The long-time employee whose credibility is based on social facilitation, knowledge of the organization information communications channels, and so forth, suddenly seems unsuited to be in a productivity-based environment.

3. The disruption of the information communications network could mean loss of friendships and a consequent decrease in morale.

4. The significant social input of nonverbal and verbal communications to the self-image and esteem of the individual can be seriously diminished.

Thus the human communication issue goes beyond the simple acceptance of telecommunications mediation for interpersonal interaction. The symbols and attitudes associated with status, control, change orientation, and the use of technology must also be considered part of the communication process.

Our data indicate that operation of a terminal, or computer-associated equipment, is considered by many managers and professionals to be beneath their status, "something that secretaries do." Automation of this sort may also signify a loss of subordinate personnel— another phenomenon associated with decreasing status. For both dimensions proper substitutes and incentives must be provided to the individual to foster adoption of the new technology.

An overwhelming obstacle to the use of computer-associated communication devices is a fear of loss of control: the individual frequently does not know "what is going on in the computer." The tendency is to revert to old-style paper shuffling and interaction methods unless systems personnel adequately communicate the capabilities of the system and explain its operation and back-up well before its implementation. Finally, these substitutes will not be adopted smoothly unless a climate for change has been communicated in the organization and the individual members are receptive to change. This climate may often be associated with fear of technology—individual obsolescence. Data we gathered from banks, insurance companies, and airlines indicate that the substitution is often successful only with an entirely new group of employees unless careful education and planning has prepared employees to accept the changes. Individuals most readily accepting these substitutes tend to be open-minded, have a good level of self-esteem, be younger than the average, be able to work independently, and are relatively new employees of the organization, with some computer experience and not in a supervisory position.

Even though telecommunication/transportation substitutes may be implemented by an authoritarian top-down command, evidence suggests that the implementation will be least costly to the organization when the human communication issues outlined are carefully accounted for.

These questions of productivity and acceptance are serious ones, and much research still remains to be done in this area. To date our own studies, and a scattered series of other studies, indicates that for properly planned systems worker productivity levels resulting from the use of telecommunications remain at least as high as, and in some cases increases over that of the traditional monolithic, central organization [11.4]. The individual organization would be expected to take advantage of this productivity increase by decreasing or limiting growth of its personnel complement for a given level of business. Yet, past history seems to indicate that where local reduction in employment has occurred new job opportunities in related economic areas have increased. The skill required for these jobs has also tended to increase. The net result is still a gain in productivity for the general working population. Unfortunately it may also cause an increasing gap in employability between skilled and unskilled workers.

An important issue in decentralization is that of enforcement of local hiring. Several alternative strategies and societal effects are possible depending on how decentralization occurs. If the satellite work centers are designed so that each is a fragmented one, performing a single function (for example, health insurance claims or policy underwriting in our case study example), then there are limited options available both to existing employees at a particular center and to prospective employees living in the area. First, when the company initially decentralizes, the employees of a fragmented center must either commute greater distances to work on the average, or move their residences to continue their jobs. Second, once the company has fragmented, local employees who move from the area must either get training for new jobs, if positions similar to their old ones are not available in the company center nearest to their new location, or must change employers. Finally, entrance level employees living in the locale of the fragmented center may be less attracted to it because of the more limited variety of positions available.

The more sophisticated dispersion approach eliminates many of these problems at the expense of requiring more sophisticated computer software and changes in management structure and methodology. If the dispersion were to occur among five or six satellite work centers, as ultimately postulated in our case study, then one would expect each center to have some representation of the major departments or functions within the company. In this case if an individual employee moved, he or she could continue his or her present job at the work site closest to the new residence. If a particular work center became too small, it could be closed down since, in our assumption of leasing office space instead of owning it, the capital investment for a center is low. If, on the other hand, a work center became too large, it could be split into two or more centers more propitiously located.

In addition to improving productivity as a result of decentralization, we (and the insurance company) anticipate that employee turnover will also decrease. Two conflicting trends result from this. The reduced turnover promotes job stability and reduces training costs. However, in most organizations, salaries tend to increase with length of service under the tacit, but not necessarily well-founded, assumption that productivity increases as well. Consequently, average wages may increase at a rate higher than the increase in productivity accruing from greater length of service.

As decentralization increases in popularity, more firms will open up offices in the regional activity centers. One consequence of this will be that the cost advantage to a firm for decentralization will tend to diminish somewhat. If urban redevelopment activities around central business districts are altered to become more attractive to clerical-level workers, some of the trend of moving residences away from the CBD may be reversed. As this occurs the wage premium now required to entice workers to come to the CBD may diminish to the point where there is no clear cost advantage in moving to a particular regional center. However, this is not expected to occur until the regional centers and the former central business district are of roughly the same size, a point that will occur only as population increases act to expand the size of the regional centers.

Some federal labor policies play an important part in the decentralization decision by the managements of many information industry firms. Specifically, current government regulations specify that each place of work is to be considered separate for the purposes of unionization. Hence a nonunionized company typically exhibits extreme reluctance to put itself in the position where individual sites can be "picked off" one by one by active union organizers, while their single, central organization has been able to resist such efforts for years.

Decentralization through telecommuting offers some intriguing possibilities for furthering equal employment opportunities, however. If the decentralization is arranged so that employment centers are located in areas with high levels of minority group population higher paying jobs will be brought to the minority areas. This is in contrast to the usual present situation in which considerable effort is expended in trying to plan the daily commute of minorities to locations offering higher paying jobs.

Two possible consequences of the location of regional work centers in minority areas can ensue. First, as the economic level of the minority employees rises, they may choose to leave the area for more desirable sections of the city in a flight similar to the middle and upper class exodus to the suburbs. Thus, the minority area centers might serve as a continuous training ground for the potential labor force of marginally functional capability. On the other hand, the more desirable prospect is that the increased influx of wages and salaries to the minority areas will allow these areas to develop themselves and become more attractive places in which to live. Both of these alternatives are drawn under the assumption that equal employment opportunity rules will be tested on a company as a whole.

Another possibility is that equal employment opportunity rules will be applied separately to each satellite work center. In this case it is easy to envision scenarios in which one ethnic group is brought into another ethnic area simply to meet local equal employment opportunity standards, thereby defeating the goal of reducing the use of transportation— unless the ethnic groups have their residences moved as well. The scenario that appears to have the most desirable features of all these possibilities is one in which the local work center in a minority area initially possesses an employee population of primarily minority workers, some of whom, as their incomes and responsibilities increase, may move to other ethnic areas of the city and vice versa. The net result after many cycles of this evolution, would be a gradual amelioration of the gross ethnic and economic imbalances endemic in U.S. urban areas.

SOCIAL IMPACTS

On a very broad scale decentralization through the use of telecommunications could have considerable impact on individuals and family groups. The creation of smaller neighborhood work centers could create more community identity, both for the individual, the family, and the business organization. With a decrease in commuting time and distance individuals would be able to spend more time with their families and friends and use healthier means of getting to work, such as bicycling and walking. The existence of local offices could, with the schedule flexibility afforded by interactive computer networks, allow much more part-time job mobility, as discussed earlier. A reduction in human frustration with traffic congestion could have beneficial effects not only on the temperament of employees but also on their productivity.

The ability of computer systems to monitor output and productivity, at least of routine jobs, could help establish a trend in the information industry toward a form of payment based on the number and the quality of jobs performed. This, in turn, could allow the faster and more efficient workers either to attain higher incomes, or to have more leisure time available. The net result of these changes could well be a favorable change in the quality of life for the individual; a change predicated on a healthier environment and a heightened feeling of identity with his or her community, family, and co-workers.

SUMMARY

Although many of the tradeoffs and impacts discussed in this and the previous chapter have been based on experimental evidence, many of them are quite speculative. We do not know which of the social effects will occur, or to what extent they may occur. Many of the earlier fears of great emotional trauma resulting from prolonged interaction with computer terminals have proved groundless in practice. Many of the questions of the proper design of the man–machine interface in an interactive computer society have yet to be answered. Much research still needs to be done. Because of the complexities of the physical and social structure of an urban area it is extremely difficult, if not practically impossible, to get a coherent and accurate picture of the possibilities for urban development. Yet we feel we have developed enough information to make some preliminary comments on the public policy questions relating to these impacts.

REFERENCES

1. U.S. Bureau of the Census. *Statistical Abstract of the United States.* Washington, D.C.: Government Printing Office, 1972, p. 740.
2. Garrett Hardin, "The Tragedy of the Commons." *Science*, Vol. 162, December 13, 1968, pp. 1243–1248.
3. John McHale. *World Facts and Trends.* New York: Collier Books, 1972, p. 17.
4. J. W. Lawrie, et al. *Terminals and the Impact on Employee Motivation.* Datamation, August, 1974, pp. 59–62. This article concluded that, although no significant long-term change in productivity could be detected in a bank using terminals, a feeling of employee identity with the company increased.

Chapter 12

Policy Implications

The previous chapters have dealt with the inherent potential of telecommunications and computer technologies for replacing transportation in many information industry functions and with the general societal impacts implicit in these capabilities. If it were not for the fact that the implications of the tradeoff in favor of telecommunications could be considerably broader than the direct effects on the types of business involved, there would be relatively little concern with public policy, except, possibly in regard to restraint of trade considerations. However, because there are so many potential effects of substituting communications for transportation, a number of public policy issues must be reviewed.

Public policy often seems to work most effectively when it acts to influence the market process. In particular we are concerned here with the telecommunications technology market process as depicted in Figure 12.1. Although this approach might be considered overly simplistic, it does serve to illustrate the ways in which public policy can influence the development and diffusion of telecommunications and computer technologies. It aslo serves as a means for emphasizing one of our fundamental hypotheses: the increase in demand for these technologies will be essentially spontaneous, since it will depend largely on individual organizational decisions, influenced primarily by market pressures rather than by government regulations.

With this as background, our examination of the policy implications of the telecommunications-transportation tradeoff develops from two fundamental questions.

1.   Who are the primary interested parties in this potential evolutionary aspect of telecommunications?

2.   What influence can they have in accelerating or retarding the technological development of telecommunications?

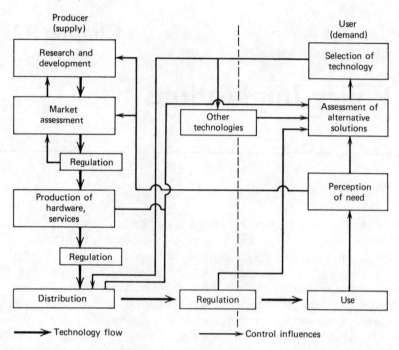

Figure 12.1 The telecommunications technology market process.

There are two main groups of interested parties: government (as representatives of the public) and business. Both of these groups are involved in the telecommunications technology market process illustrated in Figure 12.1. Both government and business organizations can be found in most of the blocks depicted there. Both government and business exert a regulatory influence on various aspects of the market process. Some of these influences are explicit while others are implicit. The influence of each of the factors in Figure 12.1 on increasing or diminishing the development of telecommunications and related computer technologies is summarized as follows.

PERCEPTION OF NEED

Business telecommunications, almost until the last decade, were limited primarily to two-way telephone conversations and the use of the teletype system to transfer messages from point-to-point. In the last decade, however, increasing numbers of businesses have begun to use computer technologies to expand, improve, and diversify their operation. Furthermore, in this same period techniques have developed for intercomputer communications, especially new applications of computer time sharing operations using remote terminals.

One key telecommunications policy decision allowed this revolution to come about. The Carterfone Case, which was argued with the Federal Communications Commission (FCC) during the latter part of the 1960s, ultimately resulted in an FCC regulation allowing devices not owned by AT&T to be connected to Bell System telephone lines, provided that the interface equipment met certain quality standards. This paved the way for the proliferation of computer time-sharing systems and terminals now appearing. As a result many business and government organizations are using telecommunications to gain access to computers of a size and power they cannot justify owning outright, or to provide more efficient use of their available computer capabilities. The enormous decreases in cost per information element in computers over the last decade have played a major part in the proliferation of computer technology. Microprocessor technology, which is now allowing the development of relatively inexpensive "smart" computer terminals, will continue this proliferation.

As information industry organizations expand and their customer bases widen, they become more dependent on the rapid transfer of information from point-to-point. This applies to both private and public sector organizations. This need is the most obvious driving force behind the telecommunications and associated computer technologies markets.

The less obvious forces leading toward wider acceptance of telecommunications and computer technologies have been discussed at some length in previous chapters. Yet these forces, taken together, appear to be often more powerful than the need for more information transfer systems. In fact, the need perceived most forcefully by many information industry firms is often the need to decentralize, not the need to adopt new and improved telecommunications and computer technologies. Only later is it seen that, if decentralization is to be effective, the organization must find convenient and economical methods for rapid point-to-point communication between its decentralized units.

At first glance it would not appear that there is much regulatory influence on this decision. Yet, aside from the Carterfone decision, there are several direct regulatory factors that can influence the decision by an organization to decentralize, thereby influencing the decision to choose telecommuting. Local zoning ordinances can restrict the potential locations for decentralized offices. If properly designed and, more important, strictly enforced, these ordinances can guide urban development into the regional center form already discussed. If the design is poor, or if the ordinances are either ignored or altered to suit the purposes of individual developers, the result can easily be continued and expanding urban sprawl.

These same land use policies can also restrict the development of new roads and highways, thereby encouraging concentration into regional centers. Various other transportation policies can reinforce the trend toward development of urban regional centers, and can reduce the perceived risk of decentralization. Some of these supporting policies are encouragement of short-range, center-oriented bus systems (for example, Dial-a-Ride, and/or jitney services), encouragement of line-haul, intercenter mass transit system developments, and discouragement of broad area mass transit systems.

Labor policy issues can have opposing effects on the decision to decentralize. Equal Employment Opportunity Guidelines make it attractive for potential employers to explore ways of getting the work to the workers in minority areas. This decision can be made by individual organizations, whereas the other alternative, development of an efficient transportation system to get minority workers to the work is out of the hands of individual organizations. On the other hand, the fear that decentralization will produce an environment leaning toward easier unionization is a significant concern to senior executives of many information industry organizations and can act to deter the process.

Energy and environmental policies can also have a complex effect on the decentralization decision. For example, present energy conservation trends toward decreasing fuel consumption of automobiles in order to decrease the use of fossil fuels logically leads toward the development of more efficient automobile engines. Yet, in the recent past, the regulations toward decreased automobile air pollution have tended to result in less efficient engines. The predominant compromise solution to date has been a consumer trend toward smaller cars and engines with various pollution-reducing devices; a trend that tends to maintain a status quo, or at least diminish the rate of increase of a sense of urgency toward telecommuting.

Decreasing the availability of automobile fuel, as mentioned before, would probably be more effective in increasing telecommuting. Decreasing the availability of fuels could be accomplished either by direct rationing (that is, by policies designed simply to slow the rate at which distilled petroleum products flow into the economy) or by diversion of our fossil resources to other uses, such as the production of plastics and other synthetic products.

This preservation of fossil resources for nonfuel uses may be a much more desirable alternative and will probably increase in popularity as other energy sources are developed (such as geothermal and various forms of solar and nuclear energies). However, nonfossil fuel resources are not expected to provide a significant portion of the national energy budget until the turn of the century. Hence energy conservation techniques such as telecommuting are much more likely to have near-term impact than will development of these new energy resources.

The central energy policy question is whether to encourage energy conservation by such means as providing tax benefits or other subsidies to individuals and organizations using telecommuting, or to discourage transportation use by the methods already discussed.

All of these policy issues can affect the demand for organizational decentralization and its consequential demand for increased use of telecommunications and computer technologies and for decreased use of transportation. But before an organization can complete its decision to decentralize, it must examine alternate means of accomplishing the decentralization in an effective way.

ASSESSMENT OF ALTERNATIVE SOLUTIONS AND SELECTION OF TECHNOLOGY

In principle several ways exist in which an organization can decentralize and still satisfy its need for rapid point-to-point communications. Written messages can be sent through the U.S. Postal Service or by courier (federal policies affect this fact by changing the cost and reliability of service). Representatives can meet with customers or other company representatives at distant locations. Finally, various forms of telecommunications can be utilized to transfer information. A primary consideration in an organization's selection of one or more of these alternatives is the cost of sending the information at a given level of effectiveness or accuracy. As we have seen, decreasing costs of telecommunications, particularly the computer-mediated communications already mentioned, have motivated a growing number of organizations to choose telecommunications solutions for their communications problems.

Another key factor in the assessment of alternative solutions to the communications need is the availability of various alternatives. Federal and local laws and other forms of nongovernmental regulation (such as a company's decision to withhold a new telecommunications product or service) can play an important part in this issue at several points. For example, if a telecommunications capability is not available to an organization at all of the locations with which it wishes to communicate (or at least at all of the major points), it may choose another alternative using transportation simply to ensure uniformity in its operations. Or, it may simply not decentralize. Failure to establish an extensive, geographically dispersed service is one of the major reasons given for the lack of success of AT&Ts Picturephone.

Failure by the industry or governments to establish uniform standards of data transmission quality and interconnection fidelity could degrade common carrier telecommunications networks enough to make them unuseable. On the other hand, government regulations that affect the availability of transportation (e.g., increasing fuel prices, or more important, direct restrictions on the availability of fuel), are causing many organizations to consider seriously the use of telecommunications, even where its initial use may be less convenient than the use of transportation. Thus various aspects of the regulatory process are an important part of the technology selection process.

MARKET ASSESSMENT, RESEARCH, AND DEVELOPMENT

In the supply sector of the market process, the first two areas to be affected by user demand are research and development (R&D) and market assessment. The interaction between these two portions of the supply process are, ideally, quite close. A potential producer of a telecommunications technology perceives or anticipates a need in the demand sector and initiates appropriate research and development. Through the R&D process, which can be extremely short or quite extended, the supplier produces a prototype for a product that is hopefully saleable.

There can be a considerable amount of government subsidy and regulatory interaction in this portion of the supply process. As the source of massive R&D funding and as a potential customer of telecommunications and computer technologies, the federal government has been a major force in the development of much of our national capability in these fields. A striking example has been the development of the ARPA network by the Department of Defense. The ARPANET is a unique and extraordinarily valuable testing ground for the development of computer interconnection techniques, teleconferencing, the "paperless" office, and related telecommunications and computer technologies. Some of the telecommunications techniques and technologies developed with ARPA support (e.g., packet switching) are now beginning to appear in the private sector as used by value-added carriers (VACs).

Although ARPA, other Department of Defense agencies, and NASA have been heavily involved in funding R&D for defense and space purposes, other federal agencies have not fully assumed the task of funding research related to the other areas we have been discussing. From our own experience we have found that no federal agency, with the possible exception of the National Science Foundation, identifies itself as having a definite, central role in supporting research or coordinating the federal role in the civil sector aspects of research in telecommunications and computer technologies. People engaged in research on some of these interstitial aspects of telecommunications are familiar with the reply from almost every federal agency that the research, while it sounds interesting, is not within the mission area of the agency being queried. Yet, because of the pervasive effects on society of these technologies, it is vital that some coherent programs be developed for exploring new uses and assessing the effects of these technologies.

Unfortunately, most businesses are unwilling or unable to take the enormous financial risks required to initiate the expensive research and development process associated with new technologies when a clear near-term market is not apparent. The possible exceptions to this general rule are AT&T, IBM, Xerox, and other "giants" of the industry (and Xerox has recently divested itself of its Data Systems operations). These firms have two key attributes that enable them to engage in a high level (in the order of $2 to $3 billion annually) of research and development. First, they devote a reasonable portion of income, typically in the order of 3 to 5%, to research and development. Second, they have a sufficiently high level of income to support diverse and innovative R&D programs. Their research programs have resulted in the continued growth of these companies, a subsequently greater share of the market, and finally, a high level of involvement in and interaction with the regulatory process.

The extensive R&D activities of these "giants" has been instrumental in creating the massive and unmatched technological base for telecommunications in the United States; it also gives them a technological base for their own form of regulation: withholding the introduction of new products until the market or competition dictates their introduction.

This latter action is in conformance with established business conservatism: do not replace existing plant and equipment before it is necessary because of wear, threat of competition, or major changes in demand.

In summary, government subsidy and regulatory factors clearly have an influence not only on the quantity, but also on the type of research and development performed in the United States. Further, these regulatory factors can be key elements in the assessment by a potential technology producer of those areas in which he is most likely to receive an adequate return on his R&D investment.

PRODUCTION AND DISTRIBUTION OF HARDWARE, SOFTWARE, AND SERVICES

It is in the production, and particularly the distribution portions of the telecommunications technology market process, that regulatory factors are most evident and direct. It is also in this area where the question as to who is regulating whom and to what end is more frequently the center of telecommunications policy discussion and litigations. One of the primary reasons claimed for establishment of the Federal Communications Commission was to ensure that telecommunication technology and services were made available to all sectors of the U.S. citizenry, whether or not the sales volume of hardware and services in a particular area justified the capital investment required to provide those services.

It is argued that firms such as AT&T require both vertical and horizontal near-monopolies in order to provide a high level of service at a low cost to all its customers (AT&T owns about 80% of the U.S. telecommunications common carriers plant) [12.1, 12.2]. The continuing provision of this high level of service includes a substantial technology research and development program, the fruits of which (e.g., the development of the transistor) often are useful far beyond the immediate interests of the corporation.

The counter argument is that the control of the market implicit in this arrangement allows the corporation to control (and presumably decrease) the rate at which new technology is diffused into the market [12.3]. This latter argument has been the central theme of most of the regulatory litigation of the past several years involving the FCC, AT&T, and various prospective developers of new technologies or services. Success of the counter argument has led to the establishment of the specialized and value-added common carriers for data transmission and the demand that AT&T divest itself of Western Electric, its hardware manufacturing capability.

It is particularly this challenged area of data transmission that has the greatest potential impact on organizations considering substitution of telecommunications for transportation. Our case study of the insurance firm indicated (Chapter 5) that the company could economically disperse its operations through the use of existing common carrier telecommunications facilities (mostly AT&T owned). However, the study also showed that the company could realize a substantial savings if it were to operate or participate in the operation of a private, wideband telecommunications network to interconnect its regional offices. Furthermore, the data transmission capabilities of the private network we considered were far greater than necessary for the company's operations. Thus if a private telecommunications common carrier were to establish the same network interconnecting the designated regional points and sell its capabilities to other firms who wished to disperse (thus distributing the costs), the savings to the individual company could be even greater.

Interestingly this type of private network, since it would interconnect locations solely within the State of California (or, in other instances, within major metropolitan areas located solely in a single state), would not, apparently, come under the jurisdiction of the Federal Communications Commission. Instead, it would be under the jurisdiction of one of more state public utility commissions or local municipal franchise boards, most of which are totally unprepared to deal with regulatory issues of this sort.

For example, FCC-regulated common carriers are normally constrained to charge a rate which, in effect, provides a large surplus income in urban areas, where the cost of plant and service per customer is low. This same rate causes a deficit in rural areas where the costs are high. The net rural cost and urban surplus are averaged by the rate structure to provide a reasonable overall profit for the carrier. In 1973 AT&T filed a tariff request with the FCC to allow "responsive pricing" wherein the rate would be proportional to the service, at least over high density interurban routes [12.4]. This request was presumably in response to the competition threatened by the specialized common carriers offering data transmission services over the same routes.

However, this interurban rate situation is different from the intraurban private network case. Since no such specialized common carrier exists at present, the issue is hypothetical, at least for the present. The noteworthy conclusion, however, is that existing telecommunications technologies and services—both those currently available from

AT&T, GTE (General Telephone and Electronics), and other common carriers, as well as those available from specialized and value-added common carriers—combined with existing computer technologies, are sufficiently low in cost to induce business to adopt more extensive use of these technologies. As transportation costs increase, their attractiveness will increase even further.

While the major regulatory issues in this area have not appeared, they will include the following problems: Who will own and who will regulate (including setting quality and interconnect standards) the special purpose, metropolitan area interconnect networks? To what extent should this type of communications activity be left to private enterprise?

Here an interesting interaction between telecommunications and land use policies is seen. If metropolitan interconnect network development were left to occur on a laissez-faire basis, allowing the carriers to be guided solely by economic considerations, the effect might be to confine the activity to the centers where the capital costs of installing the necessary transmission lines are sufficiently low. That is, the carrier would presumably seek to minimize its investment in fixed plant in order to allow more flexibility in provision of services and terminal equipment. The effect of this could be a desired tendency toward concentration of development to a small number of regional activity centers rather than the present trends of suburban spread. This is analogous to, but opposite in result from, the process whereby development (at public expense) of new roads increases urban spread.

There is another aspect to be examined in the issue of free competition in the market versus restraining or guiding development. This relates to the efficiency of the R&D process. It is clear from the success of the specialized common carriers that suitable telecommunications capability can be attained by companies that do not possess the massive R&D capability of AT&T. It is not as clear whether this success would be as great without the massive base of federal R&D support. For example, Telenet Communications Corporation, operator of a value-added network employing packet switching, was founded by the former ARPA employee who was responsible for developing the packet switching technique. It is also clear that the mortality rate of small, independent telecommunications technology and service-producing companies is high.

Another characteristic of small companies in the industry is that they tend to perform very little self-funded R&D. Since their success is often due to the manufacture of products or the provision of services that have been developed with government support or by larger firms, they frequently cease to exist when these larger resources are not available to them. Medium-to-large R&D performing firms in the industry may react to this situation by being more protective about their innovations. If the smaller firm subsequently goes out of business users of its products are thus faced with a sudden unavailability of goods and services. Meanwhile the technological brain-power responsible for the first market forays of the new company has effectively been withheld from more productive uses. This potentially chaotic situation is both inefficient and costly for the general community.

The conclusion, therefore, is that some competition is healthy, but that unbridled competition may be destructive in the long term. Therefore regulatory policy formulation in this area should be directed toward allowing relatively free competition in the provision of new technological capability (as long as new firms meet or exceed minimum performance standards) combined with requirements for at least a minimum level of economic and social responsibility on the part of firms in the industry, including a return of at least some minimum fraction of net income to R&D product improvement.

Divestment of Western Electric from AT&T can also result in a decrease in effectiveness of the development of innovative technology uses. This would result from a slowing of the interaction between the manufacturer and the laboratory (Bell Telephone Laboratories). This interaction is critical for maintaining the efficiency of technology development. The issue to be faced is whether the market freeing effects of the proposed divestiture will result in a net increase or decrease in national technological development. Will a decrease in AT&T effectiveness be outweighed by an increase in effectiveness of other firms in the industry?

SUMMARY AND RECOMMENDATIONS

The telecommunications–transportation tradeoff affects many areas of public policy. Because the technologies are often in the role of the hidden or unperceived enablers of social decisions, their development is not often seen as a policy issue. Since the effects of the technologies are pervasive, however, we must begin to consider their interrelationships more carefully.

Fortunately we are at the stage of development in the application of these technologies where a considerable amount of experimental information concerning their effectiveness in meeting many of these social and economic pressures can be gained through the marketplace.

It is in these areas that we should encourage the development of telecommunications technologies through the competitive process. At the same time, we should maintain a vigilant eye on the results of these various technological experiments to assess which do and do not portend long-term benefits to the public. Where significant reductions in energy use, diminished use of scarce resources, and greater productivity can be achieved without correspondingly great social costs of one sort or another, we should develop regulatory processes to ensure that these technologies are made available to the broadest possible segment of the public. Our processes of regulation of telecommunications should be anticipatory rather than reactive. We should plan for the development of telecommunications capabilities of increasing quality by whatever means are most likely to provide them. At present such planning does not occur in any coordinated way.

Traditionally the United States has been a nation of innovators. We have been responsible for much of the computer, telecommunications, and transportation revolution. We must now become equally innovative in adapting the uses of these technologies to changing world conditions.

REFERENCES

1. American Telephone and Telegraph Company. *Annual Report.* 1974.
2. John G. Reynolds. "12.2 Billion for Construction in '73–Up 10.2%." *Telephone Engineer and Management.* June 15, 1973.
3. Richard Gabel. "Telecommunications Interconnection: Wherefrom and Whitherto?" In *Communications Technology and Social Policy.* George Gerbner, Larry P. Gross, and William H. Melody, Eds. New York: Wiley-Interscience, 1973.
4. "AT&Ts Rate Plans Jolt the Competition." *Business Week,* March 3, 1973, p. 26.

Related Research

From the outset of the project, the research team collected and evaluated information on related projects. This literature search revealed that a great deal of research has been and is being performed on the efficacy of telecommunications and computer technologies as a substitute for certain types of face-to-face transactions. A variety of uses of these technologies have been postulated and tested, ranging from telemedicine in rural areas to intracity teleconferencing for city officials, to international scientific exchange via a computer network. The technologies considered include videophone, telephone, slow scan television, cable, and computer data communications. The literature includes studies on the attitudinal and behavioral aspects of telecommunications use, reviews of the available technology, reports on specific experimental projects, and policy studies and projections. Discussions of several of the more important studies (in terms of the USC research) follow.

RICHARD C. HARKNESS

A major compilation of previous work performed was available in a dissertation published by Richard Harkness while he was at the University of Washington [A.1]. This work also includes a preliminary systems analysis of the possibility of substituting telecommunications for transportation within a city.

Harkness examined a hypothetical city with a radial transportation network and computed the savings in miles traveled and in energy consumption for a number of alternative configurations. Specifically, he postulated a central business district supplemented by a set of satellite work centers. His calculations indicated that, for his idealized circular city, four satellites should be located symmetrically at approximately the radial distance from the city center. Additional satellites would yield increasingly marginal improvement.

Harkness was primarily concerned with the use of communications to cope with the growing number of jobs, so these increments would be dispersed from the central business district, the latter remaining at its current population level. The study is primarily theoretical; his representative information is not based on any specific city. One of the primary objectives of the USC research was to examine whether the savings predicted by Harkness could be realized in a practical situation.

PETER C. GOLDMARK AND THE "NEW RURAL SOCIETY"

Under sponsorship of the U.S. Department of Housing and Urban Development, Goldmark Communications, Inc., and a research group at the University of Connecticut are developing background information for a demonstration project in which numerous low-density rural communities communicate with each other and perform their work through various telecommunications modes. The project anticipates that a spectrum of "urban" services, facilities, and events would be available to the inhabitants of the new rural communities via telecommunications.

This research is different from the USC research in that Goldmark anticipates an ultimate "spreading" effect throughout rural areas and a radically different structure for American society; the USC research, on the other hand, is based on the premise that the existing urban structure is likely to persist, although in a modified form, at least in the near term. (It could be said that the USC and Goldmark emphases are on the near and far ends of an evolutionary process, respectively.) Working from this premise, the USC research team considered alternate modes of evolution for our cities, given the options offered by the new communications and computer technologies. The USC research is directed toward revitalization of urban areas, with central business districts evolving from special use areas into communities that blend offices, living quarters, and recreational and entertainment facilities.

One of the specific studies performed by the New Rural Society Project involved experiments with various modes of teleconferencing systems to test their relative effectiveness for business purposes. The group came to the following conclusions:

1. Conferees who were previously acquainted with each other performed better than those who were unacquainted when an audio-only system was used.

2. Conferees who were previously acquainted with each other *performed better when using an audio-only conferencing system than they did in face-to-face meetings.*

3. Complex group discussions were felt by the users to be more effective in a face-to-face mode.

4. Video systems were rated no higher than audio modes for other communications purposes.

The group, with the cooperation of a bank, the Union Trust Company, made a 6-month field test of an audio-only teleconferencing system using stereophonic sound (so that conferees could identify each other by their apparent aurally derived position) and a facsimile device for transmission of graphic information. They found the following:

Almost all participants in the trial substituted use of the system for at least 50 percent of their face-to-face meetings, and over one-third substituted teleconferencing for 80 percent or more of their face-to-face meetings. [A.2].

The participating bank felt that the costs of installing and operating the system were outweighed by more than a factor of 2 in savings associated with the elimination of travel.

BELL CANADA

The Business Planning Group of Bell Canada has been investigating the potential of using telecommunications as a substitute for interurban travel in Canada. They conclude that a potentially large market exists in Canada for this use of telecommunications, if there is public acceptance of the new mode. Researchers from Bell Canada have recently completed preliminary interviews of approximately 40,000 travelers between Canadian cities to determine public attitudes toward travel and telecommunications substitutes.

Bell Canada has also been conducting research in teleconferencing for several years. This work has been done primarily by the Business Planning Group in Montreal, under the direction of Lawrence Day.

The work has been concerned with five major areas of impact: (1) the availability of new technologies and possibilities for their applications; (2) information transfer volume, that is, definition of those transactions amenable to performance through a telecommunications systems; (3) cost-benefit analyses; (4) behavioral and attitudinal factors; and (5) ecological, environmental, and resource allocation concerns. Bell Canada has also shown considerable interest in computer augmented conferencing (CAC), which represents a merging of computer and communications systems. In the past the Business Planning Group sponsored audio teleconferences between various institutions on the problems associated with telecommunications–transportation tradeoff. They are now involved in sponsoring a series of computer-augmented conferences.

OFFICE OF EMERGENCY PREPAREDNESS

In 1972 the Office of Emergency Preparedness investigated the potential of teleconferencing as a substitute for transportation within a large government organization. Murray Turoff, former Assistant Director for Resource Analysis in the Office of Emergency Preparedness (and now Professor, Department of Computer Sciences, Newark College of Engineering), has written several articles propounding the special capabilities of teleconferencing. He favors computer-augmented conferencing and similar data network communication modes for two reasons: (1) an increased capability for group interaction and efficient communication with others; and (2) cost effectiveness. He feels that computer-augmented conferencing is particularly suited to group communication because it is asynchronous. Verbal communication, he notes, "represents a synchronous form of communication. Individual participation is sequential and under the control of the group, along with any explicit or implicit rules of order that apply . . . one may either listen or talk when allowed to" [A. 3]. Computer conferencing, on the other hand, gives the individual control over entry (talking) and reviewing (listening).

Another advantage of computer-assisted communication is the ease of reference, since each message is assigned an entry number. By using identifiers, the computer can also sort out related messages over an extended period of time and provide "clean" conversations on a particular subject. A further advantage is the ability to enter private messages, a subgroup capability which Turoff terms "whispering." Finally, computer-augmented communication permits participation over time, that is, groups need not be called together from various geographical locations, or even, as in a telephone or video conference, required to talk and/or listen at the same time. Asynchronous teleconferencing by computer permits entry and review at both a convenient time and place.

Dr. Turoff participated in a computer-augmented conferencing system called EMISARI (Emergency Management Information System and Reference Index) which operated at the Office of Emergency Preparedness. As indicated by the system name, the network was utilized primarily as a management information tool, transmitting information between parties. Although a real-time computerized conference capability existed, its use was confined to clarification of changes in reporting formats or instruction.

INSTITUTE FOR THE FUTURE

Sponsored by ARPA and the National Science Foundation, the Institute for the Future (IFF) in Menlo Park, California, has been developing a computer program called FORUM, which is designed to permit effective computer-augmented conferencing. The FORUM system provides a unique mode of remote teleconferencing. It consists of a series of machine language programs that permit users to send messages to a central file. Messages are numbered sequentially and stored. They can be retrieved by message number or other index. More important, since at one point the system was embedded in the TENEX executive of the ARPA network, messages could be sent to all conference participants who were on-line at the time of transmission. FORUM provides both a real-time capability as well as a permanent, retrievable hardcopy record.

In late January and early February, 1974, a FORUM conference was held under the sponsorship of Bell Canada. Participants "attended" from all over the United States, Canada, and England. However, the representatives to the conference did not travel to convene at a central place for a set period of time; rather, they participated through terminals, which they used at their homes and offices, accessing the conference at random times. The following is a typical set of entries, demonstrating the capability of computer-augmented conferencing to link participants across space and through time. It also illustrates the use of the technique to clarify ambiguities in terminology occuring between disciplines. The participants are, respectively, from London, England; Montreal, Canada; Menlo Park, California; and Washington,

D.C. The time notes before each entry are the log-on times referenced to Eastern Standard Time.

(88) WILLIAMS THU 31–JAN–74 3:20 AM, RE 86, I VOTE YES, BUT WOULD LIKE TO SUGGEST IN ADDITION THAT THE DEVELOPMENT OF METHODOLOGIES TO ANSWER THESE VARIOUS QUESTIONS MIGHT MERIT A TOPIC SECTION IN ITS OWN RIGHT. OFTEN OUR ANSWERS ARE ONLY AS GOOD AS OUR METHODS. RE 78, WE HAVE BRUCE CHRISTIE WITH US AT CSG, HE WAS THE NRS PSYCHOLOGIST UNTIL OCT 1973, AND IS STILL IN CLOSE TOUCH WITH THEIR WORK. I CAN CALL HIM IN AT ANY TIME. (FORUM)

(89) KOLLEN (CHRMN) THU 31–JAN–74 8:44 AM. IN REGARDS TO (86), I AGREE WITH THE STATEMENT IN GENERAL BUT WOULD LIKE TO SEE MORE ELABORATION OF POINT 3 WITHIN THIS STATEMENT. I FEEL THAT, AT LEAST FOR ME, THIS POINT IS SOMEWHAT AMBIGUOUS. IN ADDITION, IF THERE ARE OTHER PARTICIPANTS WHICH HAVE TROUBLE WITH ANY OF THE STATED AREAS OF DISCUSSION, PLEASE EXPRESS YOUR RESERVATIONS AT THIS TIME!

(90) JOHANSON THUS 31–JAN–74 9:09 AM. I AGREE WITH 88 THAT METHODS ARE CRUCIAL TO THE DISCUSSION, AND WOULD SUGGEST THAT THIS BE INCLUDED UNDER TOPIC 3. I SEE THIS AS RELATING THE TECHNICAL AND SOCIAL DIMENSIONS OF THIS CONFERENCE. THIS CAN, OF COURSE, BE MADE MORE SPECIFIC AS WE GO ALONG AND HAVE CONSIDERED THE FIRST 2 POINTS IN THE AGENDA.

(91) MORGAN THUS 31–JAN–74 9:18 AM. I THINK WE MAY HAVE PEOPLE TALKING ABOUT TWO THINGS HERE, WHEN I USED THE WORD METHODOLOGIES EARLIER IT WAS IN THE CONTEXT OF RESEARCH. I THINK THE SAME MEANING IS INTENDED BY WILLIAMS IN 88. I AM NOT SO SURE THAT THE SAME MEANING APPLIES IN (90). CLARIFICATION?

(92) JOHANSON THUS 31–JAN–74 9:29 AM. RE 91 I ALSO MEANT METHODOLOGY WITHIN THE CONTEXT OF RESEARCH.

(93) KOLLEN (CHRMN) THU 31–JAN–74 9:29 AM. RE 91 THE FORMAL AGENDA OF THE TRAVEL/COMMUNICATION TRADEOFF CONFERENCE IS AS FOLLOWS: 1. NEEDS OF TRAVEL AND WHAT TYPES OF TELECOM CAPABILITIES WOULD SUP-

PLEMENT OR SUBSTITUTE FOR THESE NEEDS. 2. HOW WE COMMUNICATE (E.G., FORMAT, CONTEXT, ETC.) SEE STATEMENT (62) FOR AN ELABORATION OF THIS POINT. 3. HOW CAN COMMUNICATIONS AND NETWORK TECHNOLOGY ENTER INTO THE PROCESS OF COMMUTING GIVEN THE UNDERSTANDING OFFERED IN POINTS 1 AND 2 ABOVE.

HUMAN SCIENCES RESEARCH, INC.

The Social Policy and Programs Branch of the Department of Communications (Canada) and the Human Sciences Research, Inc., recently completed a research project on the effectiveness of teleconferencing utilizing an audio system, an audio-graphic system, and two slightly different audio-visual systems. The researchers reported the following:

1. Careful definition of the information and communications needs of the organization should be made before selection of a teleconferencing system.

2. Telecommunications has the capability for permitting meetings that might not have been held in the absence of the telecommunications system.

3. Telecommunications is more efficient than face-to-face meetings both in permitting better decision making and in facilitating exchanges between geographically separated participants.

4. Telecommunications promotes the use of multiple inputs in a rapidly changing situation.

5. Telecommunications systems improve communications and thereby contribute to organizational effectiveness.

6. Video, although far more expensive, did not greatly improve either user receptivity or system effectiveness over the use of audio augmented by an alphanumeric display using audio bandwidths.

These conclusions support the hypothesis that a relatively inexpensive telecommunications system can effectively transmit information and, accordingly, can improve organizational efficiency. Further, such systems may offer, in some situations, unique and desirable added capabilities. The point that the system must be matched to the needs of the organization is almost a truism, but as a fundamental factor in the system's success it should be reiterated.

COMMUNICATIONS STUDIES GROUP, JOINT UNIT FOR PLANNING RESEARCH

Similar work has been performed in the United Kingdom by Alex Reid and the Communications Studies Group (CSG) of the Joint Unit for Planning Research at the University College, London. The CSG compared the effectiveness of communications by audio only and by videophone with face-to-face interactions in an attempt to ascertain the importance of the visual channel. Their pilot studies indicate that the presence of a visual channel neither facilitates nor hinders communication that is primarily transmission of information. However, when subjects are engaged in bargaining or problem solving, the visual channel is perceived as being more important.

The CSG found that subject perceptions of their interactions varied with medium type. This is important since perceptions play a role in the acceptability of a channel, and acceptability is an important part of effectiveness. In several experiments subjects displayed a lack of confidence in judgments made in audio-communications as opposed to judgments made in face-to-face interactions. However, this loss of confidence was not warranted in all cases. The Communications Studies Group suggests that classes of communications tasks, including tasks requiring judgments, may be accomplished with the same end results with or without a visual channel. The critical point is again a definition of tasks. In the design of the communications system it must be determined if visual cues are germane to the task involved. However, in most cases, Reid concluded visual links were not necessary.

NEW YORK METROPOLITAN REGIONAL COUNCIL (MRC)

Under a grant from the National Science Foundation, the New York Metropolitan Regional Council is investigating the effectiveness of video in providing expanded opportunities for interaction among nine local government complexes located at points in the greater metropolitan New York area. A two-way experimental television system was installed in 1973 to permit conferences among the various local government offices. Technically, the system consists of a central station in Manhattan and nine satellite stations which can communicate with each other through the central station.

Several important distinctions can be made between the Metropolitan Regional Council experiment and the ones discussed previously. First, the MRC system is not designed to replace functions previously performed by other means, but rather to increase productivity by offering a new spectrum of functions that would not be performed otherwise. Second, the system is not being tested for effectiveness against an existing system; rather, its effectiveness will be tested through user response. If the users indicate that the system effectively increased interaction among the nine government offices, then the system will be judged favorably.

CONFRAVISION

Another system meriting mention is Confravision, operated by the United Kingdom Post Office. A similar system is in use in Canada under the Department of Communications. Confravision is a television system permitting city-to-city meetings between London, Bristol, Birmingham, Manchester, and Glasgow. Television studios in each city are specifically arranged for business meetings, and as many as five people can be seen on the screen simultaneously by the viewer. Stereo sound permits easy speaker identification. Charts, diagrams, models, and so forth can be displayed by use of a separate camera. The system is self-operated by the participants to ensure privacy.

SUMMARY

1. INFORMATION IS AMENABLE TO TRANSFER BY TELECOMMUNICATIONS.

Most experiments have indicated that a nonvisual (audio) link is sufficient for the rapid and effective transfer of routine information. In some experimental cases video was felt to be more effective when the interactions involved problem solving, bargaining, or other confrontations where nuances of expression are more critical. Studies reaching such conclusions, however, did not include effectiveness measurements on computer-augmented conferencing systems like FORUM or EMISARI which, through their asynchronous nature, encourage greater interaction, more open and rapid response, and nuances of verbal, if not tonal or facial, expression. Such systems also provide the capability for hard copy retrieval and reference messages. At this time no experiments have been performed to measure these capabilities in an actual conferencing situation where both routine and theoretical information are exchanged. Neither have computer-augmented and audio conferencing systems been studied together, adding the possibility of including tonal nuances in the information transfer process.

2. TRANSFER OF INFORMATION VIA TELECOMMUNICATIONS IS FELT TO BE EFFECTIVE.

All studies performed to date have supported the effectiveness of transfer of information by telecommunications. User support increases through time and through additional use. Again, the data is developed primarily for audio-only and video systems. No comparative experiments have been performed in this regard for computer-augmented conferences where several types of information were being transmitted. No effectiveness studies have been performed for clerical level workers; such studies are long overdue, particularly in light of recent advances in terminal design and natural language programs.

3. SYSTEM NEEDS MUST BE DEFINED PRIOR TO SELECTION OF THE APPROPRIATE CONFIGURATION.

This statement may appear simplistic, but every study to date has stressed the importance of carefully defining information flows and communication requirements. Without such definition the system may not be appropriate and therefore would be ineffective. The analysis of information industries and the case studies presented in the preceding chapters were predicated, to a large degree, upon the need to identify, by means of communications audits, the basic formal and informal communication needs and task parameters of a major segment of the white-collar labor force. Such definition, in turn, permitted estimation of the possible impact of telecommunications as a substitute for transportation.

A communications audit is essentially a formal means, using questionnaires and interviews, of identifying the communication paths, information content of messages, modalities of communication (e.g., face-to-face, telephone, letter, computer data entry, or retrieval, etc.), roles of the participants, and frequency of communication of an organization. Quite often a communications audit reveals entirely different communications paths and uses than those envisioned by the management of the organization.

REFERENCES

1. R. C. Harkness. *Communications Substitutes for Travel: A Preliminary Assessment of their Potential for Reducing Urban Transportation Costs by Altering Office Location Patterns.* Ann Arbor: University Microfilms, 1973.

2. Kay Kohl, Thomas G. Newman, and Joseph F. Tomey. "Facilitating Organizational Decentralization through Teleconferencing." *IEEE Transactions on Communications,* Vol. COM–23, No. 10, October, 1975, pp. 1098–1103.

3. Murray Turoff. "Human Communication via Data Networks." *Computer Decisions.* January, 1973, pp. 25–29.

Interviewer_____   Call #1____
Phone # Called_____   2____
Date_____   3____
Time_____   Subject Identification   Columns
_____   1–3

Hello. I am from the Annenberg School of Communications at the University of Southern California. We'd like to ask you a few questions about your use of radio and television and other issues. We'd appreciate the most accurate answers you can give. You are contributing to important scientific research. Of course, all responses are anonymous.

First, some questions about the mass media.

1. How do you get most of your information about what's going on in the world today?
   1____Newspapers   2____Radio
   3____TV   4____Magazines   4____
   5____People

2. How often do you read a *newspaper*?
   1____Every day
   2____4–5 times a week
   3____2–3 times a week
   4____About once a week
   5____Less than once a week
   6____Never   5____

3. On the average, during *one* week day (Monday–Friday), how long do you listen to the radio?
   (please code in minutes)_____   6–8____

4. In general, *why* do you listen to the radio?

   _____   9–10_____

   (List first response only)

5. Now I'm going to read you a statement; please supply
   one response you feel completes the statement.
   "Excluding news, weather, sports, and traffic reports,
   radio is helpful to me in my everyday life by providing
   me with useful information about . . ."

   _____   11–12_____

   (List first response only)

6. What useful information would you like to hear on the
   radio that you don't get now?

   _____?   13–14_____

   . . . and on television_____?   15–16_____

7. What percentage (or part) of your conversations with
   other people during the day include something learned
   from each of the following media?

   Radio_____   17–18_____

   Television_____   19–20_____

The following question pertains to public service messages
that are announced over radio and television.

8. *Community public service* messages tell you about
   events going on in town, school closings, job opportunities, medical treatment at local clinics, etc. Has any
   of this type of community information helped you make
   a decision recently?

                                        1_____No

   What decision? (Describe):_____←2_____Yes   21_____

9. If so, was it radio public service information that was
   more useful, or television public service information?

   1_____Radio

   2_____Television   22_____

10. *General public service* advertisements are messages
    which tell you about fire prevention, buckling your
    seat belt, drug abuse, a cancer check up and a check,
    etc. Have any messages like this influenced your be-
    havior?

                                        1_____No

    What behavior? (Describe):_____←2_____Yes   23_____

11. If so, were television public service announcements more useful to you, or the radio public service announcements?
    1____Radio
    2____Television   24____

12. On the average, during *one* week day (Monday-Friday) how long do you watch TV?
    (Please code in minutes)_____   25-27____

13. How recently did you do some reading in a magazine?
    1____Today/yesterday
    2____A few days ago
    3____A week ago
    4____Longer
    5____Never   28____

14. Are any of the phones in your home touch-tone (push button)?
    1____No (ask if available; if so, code #2)
    2____Touch-tone not available where I live
    3____Yes   29____

15. Do you currently subscribe to cable television?
    1____No
    2____No, not available in my area
    3____Don't know if it is available in my area
    4____Yes
    5____Canceled subscription
    6____Don't know what it is. (If respondent doesn't   30__
    know, skip to question 17.)

16. Assume for the moment you subscribe to cable TV, whether or not you actually do. Assume it is a two-way system; that is, it allows you to receive sound and TV pictures as well as send them to someone else.

    Now, if you could afford it, how much would you be willing to pay per month for the following services, if they were available to you in *your home* as additions to your cable TV service? (Please answer in dollars.)

    How much extra would you pay per month

    $_____ . . . to take high school courses, college
    (per month)   courses, or adult education for credit at
                     home?   31-33____

Would you purchase this service if it were available now?

1____No

2____Yes   34____

3____Don't know

$_____   . . . to do your shopping at home.   35–37____

(per month)   Would you purchase this service if it were available now?

1____No

2____Yes   38____

3____Don't know

$_____   . . . for entertainment such as first run mov-

(per month)   ies and special sports events in your

                    home?   39–41____

Would, you purchase this service if it were available now?

1____No

2____Yes   42____

3____Don't know

$_____   . . . for medical consultation and diagnosis

(per month)   in your home?   43–45____

Would you purchase this service if it were available now?

1____No

2____Yes   46____

3____Don't know

$_____   . . . to do your banking from home?   47–49____

(per month)   Would you purchase this service if it were available now?

1____No

2____Yes   50____

3____Don't know

$_____   . . . to perform civic and state functions

(per month)   such as voting and driver's license re-

                    newal at home?   51–53____

Would you purchase this service if it were available now?

1____No

2____Yes   54____

3____Don't know

$_____   . . . to visit friends and relatives from your
(per month)   home?   55–57_____
Would you purchase this service if it were
available now?
1_____No
2_____Yes   58_____
3_____Don't know

$_____   . . . for access to print media such as maga-
(per month)   zines and newspapers from your home?
                                                       59–61_____
Would you purchase this service if it were
available now?
1_____No
2_____Yes   62_____
3_____Don't know

$_____   . . . for access to information such as social
(per month)   security information or library books
                from your home?   63–65_____
Would you purchase this service if it were
available now?
1_____No
2_____Yes   66_____
3_____Don't know

$_____   . . . for self improvement or special instruc-
(per month)   tion such as how to build a cabinet or
                how to care for plants?   67–69_____
Would you purchase this service if it were
available now?
1_____No
2_____Yes   70_____
3_____Don't know

$_____   . . . to do your job from home?   71–73_____
(per month)   Would you purchase this service if it were
available now?
1_____No
2_____Yes   74_____
3_____Don't know

Now, we would like to ask you some questions about the way
you travel to work.

17.   First, are you presently employed?

1____No (If not, skip to question 34)
2____Yes   75____

18. What is your occupation?_____
_____
                                                                76–78____

19. How many hours per week are you employed?_____
                                                                79–80____

20. About how much *time* does it take you to get from your
home to work and back?
(Please code in minutes)_____   4–6____

21. About how many *miles* is it from your home to work
and back?_____   7–9____

22. What mode of transportation do you use most often in
getting from your home to work?.
1____Car
2____Car pool
3____Bus
4____Taxi
5____Bicycle
6____Motorcycle
7____Walk
8____Other:_____   10____
    (Specify)

23. How many automobiles do you have immediate access to?_____   11____

24. On the average, how often do you commute (traveling
back and forth to work) from your place of employment
to home and back?
1____Everyday   2____4–5 times a week
3____2–3 times a week   4____Once a week
5____Never   12____
6____Other (please specify)_____

R   In answering the following questions, imagine that you
have a 6-inch ruler, where
1 means *strongly disagree,*   *2* means *disagree,*
3 means *mildly disagree,*   *4* means *mildly agree,*
5 means *agree,* and *6* means *strongly agree.*

Now, using this scale of 1 to 6, how do you feel about the following statements?

25. Commuting (traveling back and forth to work) is a necessary evil.
1	2	3	4	5	6
SD	D	MD	MA	A	SA

    13____

26. Commuting is a useful interlude between home and work.
6	5	4	3	2	1
SA	A	MA	MD	D	SD

    14____

27. I spend too much time commuting.
1	2	3	4	5	6
SD	D	MD	MA	A	SA

    15____

28. I need to commute in order to live where I live.
6	5	4	3	2	1
SA	A	MA	MD	D	SD

    16____

29. I need to commute to have the job that I have.
1	2	3	4	5	6
SD	D	MD	MA	A	SA

    17____

30. Which *one* of the following statements best describes your feelings about commuting?
    1____It takes up too much of my time
    2____It takes too much of my effort
    3____I feel it is a waste of money

    18____

ASK ONLY IF OCCUPATION PROVIDED IS NOT MANUAL (use judgment):

31. If it were possible to perform your job in a place closer to home, which would you prefer?

    ____To continue working in the place I presently do (skip to question 33).

    ____To do my work (same job) in a location close to my neighborhood all of the time.

    ____To do my work (same job) in a location close to my neighborhood some of the time.

    ____To be able to do my work from my home all of the time.

    ____To be able to do my work from my home some of the time.

    19____

32. If you had the option of doing your job in a location closer to your home, how much if anything, would you pay for this option?

_____Nothing additional.

_____About what I now pay per month for commuting, including car upkeep, replacement, gasoline, etc.

_____More than what I now pay per month.

_____Less than what I now pay per month.   20_____

33. Is "mass transit" (e.g. bus, train) available near your home that you could take back and forth to work?

_____No   21_____

_____Yes

R   In answering the following questions imagine you have a 6-inch ruler, where

6 means *strongly agree*   5 means *agree*

4 means *mildly agree*   3 means *mildly disagree*

2 means *disagree*   1 means *strongly disagree*

Using this scale of 1 to 6, how do you feel about the following statements?

34. I like to try new products from the supermarket.

1	2	3	4	5	6	22_____
SD	D	MD	MA	A	SA	

35. There is usually only one right answer to most questions.

6	5	4	3	2	1	23_____
SA	A	MA	MD	D	SD	

36. Television is a vast wasteland with no potential.

1	2	3	4	5	6	24_____
SD	D	MD	MA	A	SA	

37. Most ideas I hear about these days are not worth taking the time to learn about.

6	5	4	3	2	1	25_____
SA	A	MA	MD	D	SD	

38. In general I enjoy shopping.

1	2	3	4	5	6	26_____
SD	D	MD	MA	A	SA	

39. In person (face to face) communication is important when I purchase a low-expense item (e.g., toothpaste).

6	5	4	3	2	1
SA	A	MA	MD	D	SD

27_____

40. In person communication is important when I purchase a moderately expensive item (e.g., portable television).

1	2	3	4	5	6
SD	D	MD	MA	A	SA

28_____

41. In person communication is important when I purchase a highly expensive item (e.g., new automobile).

6	5	4	3	2	1
SA	A	MA	MD	D	SD

29_____

Please complete the following sentences.

42. In general, I feel the most satisfactory aspect of shopping is_____

30–31_____

43. In general, I feel the most unsatisfactory aspect of shopping is_____

32–33_____

Now we would like to ask you some questions about yourself.

44. What is your age?
   1_____15–19 years
   2_____20–24 years
   3_____25–29 years
   4_____30–34 years
   5_____35–39 years
   6_____40–over

34_____

45. What is *your* (considering only yourself) approximate gross annual income?
   1_____   0– 4,999
   2_____   5,000– 9,999
   3_____10,000–14,999
   4_____15,000–19,999
   5_____20,000–24,999
   6_____25,000–29,999
   7_____30,000–34,999
   8_____35,000–39,999
   9_____40,000 or more

35_____

46. What is the occupation of the chief wage earner in your house?_____
                                                          .
                                                        36–38_____

47. What is your marital status?
    1____Single
    2____Married
    3____Widowed
    4____Divorced
    5____Other   39_____

48. How many years of education have you had?_____
                                                       40–41_____

49. Do you live in
    1____A room you rent
    2____An apartment you rent
    3____A house you rent
    4____A condominium you own
    5____A house you own
    6____With parent, guardian
    7____Other_____   42_____
              (specify)

50. (Do not ask the following unless impossible to ascertain)
    Sex of Respondent
    ____Male   43_____
    ____Female

Thank you for participating in this project. We appreciate your help.

Index